FUNNY,
YOU DON'T LOOK
AUTISTIC

A COMEDIAN'S GUIDE TO LIFE ON THE SPECTRUM

MICHAEL McCREARY

annick press
toronto • berkeley

© 2019 Michael McCreary
Edited by Paula Ayer
Cover and design by Paul Covello
Author photos by Ming Joanis, A Nerd's World, Toronto

Credits:
Conversational flow chart on page 83 credited to Nashama Mohamed.
Photos on pages 53, 114, and 148 credited to Susan McCreary and the McCreary family, with photo on page 148 shared with permission of Dr. Temple Grandin.

Annick Press Ltd.

We acknowledge the support of the Canada Council for the Arts and the Ontario Arts Council, and the participation of the Government of Canada/la participation du gouvernement du Canada for our publishing activities.

Cataloging in Publication

McCreary, Michael, 1996-, author
   Funny, you don't look autistic : a comedian's guide to life on the spectrum
/ Michael McCreary.

Issued in print and electronic formats.
ISBN 978-1-77321-257-9 (softcover).--ISBN 978-1-77321-260-9 (HTML).--
ISBN 978-1-77321-259-3 (PDF)

   1. McCreary, Michael, 1996- --Juvenile literature. 2. Autistic people--
Canada--Biography--Juvenile literature. 3. Comedians--Canada--Biography--
Juvenile literature. 4. Autistic people in the performing arts--Canada--
Juvenile literature. I. Title.

RC553.A88M43 2019   j616.85'8820092   C2018-905054-3
                                                    C2018-905055-1

Published in the U.S.A. by Annick Press (U.S.) Ltd.
Distributed in Canada by University of Toronto Press.
Distributed in the U.S.A. by Publishers Group West.

Printed in China

www.aspiecomic.com
www.annickpress.com

Also available as an e-book.
Please visit annickpress.com/ebooks.html for more details.

For Matthew

CONTENTS

INTRODUCTION 1

PART 1:
PORTRAIT OF THE ASPIE
AS A YOUNG MAN 4

1 OBLIGATORY ORIGIN STORY 9

2 SENSES CONSENSUS CAN SENSE US 17

3 THE ELEMENTARY SCHOOL DOORSTOP 25

4 BREAKING MY LEGS 33

5 THE FUNISHER: VOL. 1 47

PART 2:
EVERYONE HAS AN ANIME PHASE 58

6 MICHAEL BEGINS: THE SEARCH FOR APPROVAL 63

7 I FOUGHT THE LAW,
AND THE LAW CALLED MY PARENTS 71

8 SOCIALLY AWKWARD MAN 81

9 CINEMA du AUTISM 90

10 SAY (LITERALLY) ANYTHING 101

11 THE QUEST FOR IMMORTALITY 109

PART 3:
STIM CITY   120

12 GOOD COP, TRANSIT COP   125

13 HERE TODAY, IMPROV TOMORROW   133

14 THE TEMPLE GRANDIN SAGA   146

15 THE BROTHERS STIM   152

16 GENERATOR 2: JUDGMENT DAY   157

EPILOGUE   165

ACKNOWLEDGMENTS   167

AUTISM RESOURCES   169

Introduction

Hello! I'm Michael and I do stand-up comedy about being on the autism spectrum. Those two things don't sound like they should go together, but comedy's all about breaking the ice on topics that people are too scared to talk about.

I was diagnosed with autism at the age of five. I wasn't diagnosed as a comedian until much later, though I always loved to perform and make people laugh. When I started doing stand-up in my teens, I realized that I could use comedy to help demystify autism and break down stereotypes. Being autistic has its challenges, sure, but it's not all PSAs of empty swings blowing in the wind set to Sarah McLachlan music. There's plenty to laugh about, too.

People responded to what I was doing, and soon I went from performing in schools and church basements to bigger venues: universities, comedy clubs, conference centers, and even Toronto's famous Massey Hall. I toured Canada from coast to coast and was interviewed on national radio and TV. It was clear that the world had an appetite for autism-based humor.

Maybe you know someone with autism. In fact, you probably do, even if you don't know it. It might be a friend, someone in your family, or the kid who sits behind you in class who can't stop jiggling his leg (probably him). Maybe you're curious about what autism is, or you're seeking a deeper understanding so you can better support the people in your life.

Or maybe you're somewhere on the autism spectrum yourself. If so, congratulations! You are part of the 1.5 percent. Take solace in knowing you're not alone.

Either way, if you're looking for a comprehensive and detailed examination of autism and its myriad workings in the brain, this book you're holding is *definitely* not it. Put it down and pick up something that wasn't written by a comedian.

This is also not a book about some universal experience of "being autistic." Everyone with autism spectrum disorder (ASD) is different, and I believe I can speak for all of us when I say that I shouldn't speak at all.

What you will find here is my own story of navigating life, school, friendship, love, and amateur theater as a person who happens to have ASD. Along the way, I hope to provide some insight based on my own experiences, and conversations with other people, into what being autistic is about. And if you ever figure me out, I want an explanation.

Whether you're on the spectrum or not, I hope that you'll be able to relate to my struggles and triumphs,* and that we can laugh together at all the quirks and awkward moments that come with being human.

I met a woman recently and happened to mention that I am autistic. She responded, "That's ridiculous, you're doing great!"

I don't believe the terms are mutually exclusive.

Now is probably a good time to talk about how people with ASD like to refer to themselves. Some autistic people prefer person-first language: "a person with autism." Others prefer to put the identity first: "autistic person." I believe that people on both sides want to emphasize the value and worth of the individual. No matter what the person's point of view, it's important to respect their choice of terms.

Personally, it doesn't matter to me if someone says I'm autistic or that I have autism. They both mean the same thing in my eyes, and I use both terms. My choice at any point depends on what makes the sentence flow better and provides the clearest meaning. Over the course of this book, I'll be using these terms interchangeably.

So, remember, if you've met one person with autism (or autistic person), I hope it's Dan Aykroyd. He's a Ghostbuster!

Cheers,

Michael

*A note to my non-autistic readers: As you embark on this journey through my ASD mind, there's a high likelihood that you'll find at least some of my experiences relatable. Should this occur to you, take a deep breath and put down the Buzzfeed quiz–it doesn't mean you're autistic. People with ASD aren't aliens, and we have many of the same thoughts and feelings as anyone else; the difference is in the intensity of those feelings and the degree to which they affect our functioning. Remember that only a professional can properly diagnose someone with ASD.

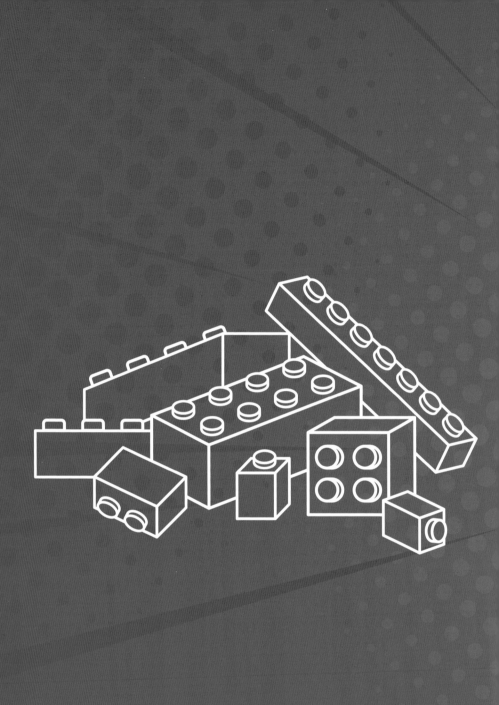

PART 1

PORTRAIT
of the
ASPIE
AS A YOUNG MAN

Growing up is tough for anyone.

But when you've been diagnosed with autism, it's an extra challenge. You have to deal with the negative perceptions and misunderstandings other people have about you, all at an age when you probably can't even spell "autism" yet. This means you need to figure out your own strengths and weaknesses and how you're going to use them. That part took me a bit of trial and error to get right.

Our saga begins with an insufferable, catchphrase-spouting toddler straight out of a network sitcom and continues into the evolution of a hardened, vengeful preteen straight out of a gritty cable drama. (There's a happy ending, I promise.) You'll also meet my family—itself a microcosm of the variety of thought patterns and behaviors that characterize the autism spectrum.

But first, one of the most formative experiences in a young autistic person's life: getting a diagnosis.

Chapter 1

OBLIGATORY ORIGIN STORY

Maybe it was the socks.

When I was a kid, I hated wearing them. I would be out walking with my folks and suddenly, I'd scream, "THERE'S A LUMP AND A CLUMP IN MY SHOE!"

They'd take off the shoe, assuming I had gotten a pebble or something stuck inside, but nothing was there. It was just the stitching on the inside of the sock that had wedged itself underneath my toes and was driving me nuts.

I couldn't wear short-sleeved shirts, either. The change in temperature from my upper arm—covered in fabric and warm—to my forearm—completely exposed and cold—felt too great. The sensory difference threw me off, and I'd have a meltdown if someone tried to put one on me.

Or maybe it was the fact that I didn't talk until I was nearly three. Then, when I finally did, I spoke exclusively in movie quotes. I was obsessed with movies from a young age and didn't discriminate in my tastes: I'd quote everything from *Casablanca* to *The Country Bears*. I didn't really understand the words I was saying—I just liked the way they sounded. So, in the McCreary home, it was a bit like living in an episode of *Full House*. I'd always be ready with a punchline:

DAD: Miiiiiiiii-chael, who put a kickball through the window?

ME: Round up the usual suspects!

(Cue theme song, executive producer credits; fade to black.)

Whatever it was that led my parents to think, "Something's up with this kid," I'm grateful. Because most kids, frankly, are weird. Their instinct when they see a decrepit cardboard box is to run inside it and say, "It's a rocket ship!" That's pretty weird, but society's fairly accepting of a moderate level of weirdness in kids. So I must have been exceptionally strange in my behavior to raise alarms.

That being said, my folks had good reason to be concerned. My younger brother, Matthew, had just been diagnosed as autistic. Even though he and I were very different in our behavior from early on, my mom and dad had to wonder, "Could this be what's going on with Michael, too?"

And that was how I ended up in a psychologist's office at age five. My folks hoped this would give them answers, but for the time being, it only seemed to raise more questions about me.

Here was the plan: My folks were going to take me to a psychologist in the city who specialized in child behavior. The doctor would ask me some questions, then he would ask them some questions, and we would all answer them politely. The doctor would then give me a diagnosis that would explain all of my problems, and my folks and I could then move on with our lives. Simple. Only it didn't turn out that way. If I'm being honest, it went more like a scene out of the horror movie *The Omen*.

Everything seemed normal when we arrived at the doctor's office. My folks were characteristically nervous about me, but I was well-behaved. We hadn't spent more than ninety seconds out in the lobby when the receptionist corralled me and my folks into a tiny, beige room. She told us, "The doctor will be with you in five minutes," and left.

That was just enough time for me to hop off the chair, rip the curtains off the wall, and completely ransack the room as my parents sat in stunned horror.

When the doctor opened the door, I was sitting in the middle of the chaos, smiling and twiddling my thumbs. All I needed was a cat to stroke, and my Bond-villain aesthetic would have been complete.

Even at the time, I don't think I understood why I did this. Acting out in that way wasn't typical for me. Maybe I felt like I was being ignored, and it was a cry for attention. Whatever the reason, the doctor had made his diagnosis:

"Well, he's a tricky one."

For people with autism, just getting a diagnosis can be the biggest struggle. Once you have it, a whole world of possible treatments and coping strategies opens up. But until you have it, you're in the dark. And that's where my parents were with me.

Autism Defined

The DSM-5 sounds kind of like a spy organization or a multilane highway. It's actually a book called the Diagnostic and Statistical Manual, created by the American Psychiatric Association. In 2013 they put out the fifth edition, hence the name DSM-5. Basically, it's the go-to book for doctors and mental-health professionals in North America. The DSM-5 defines autism as a "triad of impairments" that presents challenges in three areas:

1. Social interaction

2. Communication

3. Repetitive behaviors

Over the years, there have been a lot of different terms used to define people on the spectrum, including pervasive developmental disorder, high-functioning autism, and Asperger's syndrome. As of 2013, there are no distinctions. You either have autism or you don't, and an autistic person is said to have autism spectrum disorder (ASD).

Today, society has a firmer understanding of how autism can present itself in a multitude of ways, but back in 2001, there was still a very rigid framework for what would count as "autistic behavior." Because I wasn't meeting the conventional criteria, it was hard for doctors to recognize what was going on with me. My folks had to keep up the search for someone who could give us some answers.

> **For people with autism, just getting a diagnosis can be the biggest struggle.**

My second try at getting assessed has gone down in infamy as the Lego Incident. This one: not my fault.

In my many years of visiting psychiatric offices, I've noticed that they all look pretty much the same: beige walls, beige carpet. But the second doctor's office looked more like a Salvador Dalí painting. There was no melting clock, but something seemed a bit off about the room. It confused and upset me. I was also on edge because this time around, the receptionist had insisted I go in to see the doctor alone, reassuring my parents with the phrase: "Don't worry, she's great with kids." Which, at the time, I should have read as code for: "She eats children."

The one solace in that situation was that in the center of the room there was a giant pile of Lego. It was the new *Attack of the Clones*-themed Lego, too. I finally built up the courage to approach the mound when a voice shattered the silence: "You can't play with it yet!"

The doctor—henceforth referred to as the Lego Lady—emerged from the shadows with a proposition. "If you can answer every single one of my questions, you can play with the Lego."

Now, here was my problem: at age five, I didn't really get the meaning behind words. Not just specific words; all words. When I spoke in movie quotes, I didn't necessarily know what I was saying; I just liked the way it sounded. So when someone said to me, "Answer a question," I thought that meant I could give literally any answer.

We launched into the Q&A. She asked me the first question, and I crowed at her like Peter Pan. She asked me the second question, and I clucked like a chicken. I thought I was doing great. Things continued on this way, with my "answers" having absolutely nothing to do with what she asked me.

Finally, I finished the test, which took much longer than it needed to. I'd been thinking about the Lego the whole time and I couldn't wait any longer.

I said, "Do I get to play with the Lego now?"

She bellowed, "No! You took too long!"

I was devastated. I had *failed* my neurological assessment. I didn't think it was possible to do that!

What Causes Autism?

There's a lot of speculation as to what causes autism. Much of it is pretty silly and baseless. The truth is, we don't know the exact causes of autism, though research points to a mix of genetic and environmental factors. Personally, I don't care so much about the cause; the fact is, people with ASD are here, and a more interesting question to me is what we can do to support them.

THIS WEEK'S CAUSE OF AUTISM

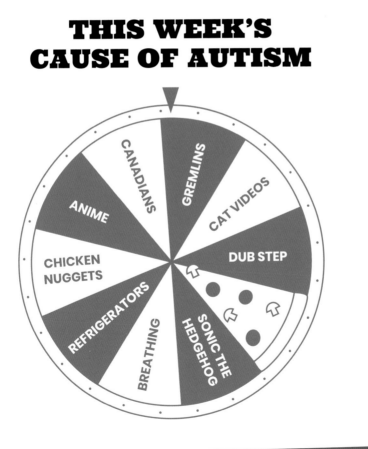

We moved on to the third psychologist, whom I'll call Dr. S. I think I'd learned some things from my two earlier experiences. I'd learned to be compliant. And I'd learned that sometimes adults just hate kids. This time around, for obvious reasons, my parents insisted they come along.

This doctor was different, though. He was less clinical and never interjected. In fact, he was more than willing to listen to what I had to say, even if all I had to say was a weird clucking sound. If the Lego Lady was Anjelica Huston from *The Witches*, Dr. S. was more like Richard Attenborough from the original *Jurassic Park*. Half an hour flew by, and then he came back with a diagnosis: autism spectrum disorder.

My diagnosis was a life-changing moment—for my folks. As for me, well, I was five years old. I just wanted to get out of there and rent *Walking with Dinosaurs* from the library, not listen to this doctor who was saying things I couldn't really comprehend. In hindsight, I wish I had been more grateful. That diagnosis would end up helping me more than I could've imagined. It was going to help me navigate school, and understand myself, and eventually figure out my place in the world.

So it was a life-changing moment for me, too—I just didn't realize it yet.

Chapter 2

SENSES CONSENSUS
CAN SENSE US*

My family has never lacked for colorful characters. The McCrearys, on my dad's side, are a family of sportsmen. Most of my forebears were born in the tiny village of Sundridge, Ontario, and most of them went on to become National Hockey League stars. My father, no slouch on the ice himself, made a name for himself playing hockey in Europe before coming home to help run the family business. He met my mother in the late 1980s. She was a nurse, a hairdresser, and the daughter of a man whose claim to fame was punching former Beatle John Lennon in the face. Together, they spawned three boys: one who hates sports (the eldest), one who loves the Beatles (the youngest), and one who stuck a candy banana up his own nose (me).

Growing up in Orangeville, Ontario, a quaint, historic town about an hour outside of Toronto, we might have seemed like

* Say it three times fast.

the picture of normalcy. If two out of the three of us were autistic, well, that was just part of our normal, too.

Frankly, I'm not surprised that my little brother and I ended up on the spectrum. Our folks are both neurotypical, but if you smooshed their quirks together, you could see how they would produce an autistic child.

How Neurotypical!

In the ASD community, "neurotypical" (sometimes abbreviated NT) is the word used to describe people who are neurologically typical, meaning they aren't on the autism spectrum and don't have any other disabilities or differences that affect how their brains function. Tip: try using it instead of "normal."

I inherited my mother's anxiety and my father's anal-retentiveness. Matthew inherited my mother's impulsiveness and my father's obsessive love of *The Commitments* soundtrack. But while we shared the same diagnosis, the two of us were about as far apart on the autism spectrum as it's possible to be.

When I was first diagnosed with ASD, I didn't feel that different from other kids. But I did know one thing: my senses were heightened. Kind of like Daredevil, if he sucked.

My socks and the tags in my clothes continued to drive me crazy, but there were other things, too. Chewing sounded louder to me. Axe Body Spray smelled worse. And I could not do crowds. My dad took me to my first hockey game when I was six. I can't remember who was playing, but I'll never forget the crowd's cheers after the home team scored. I crumpled to the floor. Given my line of work now, that wouldn't go over so well, but at the time, I couldn't help it. I was having a sensory overload, which is what happens when there's too much stimulation coming at you at once.

Noise was a particular issue for me. More specifically, a sudden burst of noise. I've gotten better at managing my sensory stress over the years, but if you can relate to my hockey-game meltdown, here are a few measures you can take to help with your own and other people's stresses:

- When you're working, set up a space with dividers on each side. Cardboard will be your best friend. Pillow forts work, too.

- For those sensitive to bright light, try wearing sunglasses with tinted lenses.

- If you're sensitive to noise, always bring earplugs or headphones with you wherever you go.

- Some autistic people actually like crowded, noisy places. If that's you or someone you know, try working more noise into your life. Take up drumming. Become a DJ!

- You can help out your family and friends with super-smelling powers by showering regularly and easing off the Axe Body Spray. On the other hand, if you have Aspie friends who love strong smells, go nuts with it!

Meltdown vs. Tantrum

There's a common misconception that a meltdown and a tantrum are the same thing. Actually, the rationale for each one is quite different. A meltdown is an autistic person's involuntary reaction to something they can't control or understand. For example: "In class today, some guy kept rubbing two pieces of foam together. The sound made my skin crawl, and I lost it." A tantrum, on the other hand, is a fit that comes from wanting something but not getting it: e.g., "What?! The karaoke bar doesn't do reservations on Friday? Hulk Smash!"

After the hockey incident, my folks were especially concerned about my noise sensitivity, as our family had been invited to see the stage version of *The Lion King* in Toronto. Despite their reservations, they persevered, with whiny young Michael in tow.

The night got off to a bad start. We went out for dinner before the show, and in the restaurant, I was already having sensory issues. This was only exacerbated when I stupidly nabbed a hot chicken wing off a man's plate (a total stranger, mind you) and bit into it like an unruly barbarian. A barbarian who could not handle anything hotter than medium.

By the time we got to the theater, I was a mess. My mouth was burning. My eyes were watering. And the show was about to start. I was a ticking time bomb waiting for a noise to set me off. My folks sat there with bated breath, preparing themselves for the moment *The Lion King*'s iconic opening notes would turn me into an blubbering puddle.

And I must have surprised the heck out of them. Maybe it was the awe-inspiring power of song. Maybe that chicken wing had burned off all of my taste buds. For whatever reason, I was quiet ... at least until the song ended. The second the opening number finished, I screamed, "Do it again!"

The audience erupted in laughter, and I sat there, confused that the actors weren't listening to me.

While my hypersensitivity was throwing a wrench in my parents' social life, my brother Matthew was having the opposite problem: it turned out he was hyposensitive, meaning his senses were too dull. He couldn't feel heat and cold like other people, which meant my parents had to watch that he didn't burn or freeze himself. And because he was so undersensitive to sensory information, he needed to seek out stimulation. He loved loud noises, which was convenient because we lived right next to a highway. Truck horns were his favorite. (Other people who are hyposensitive might like spicy foods or strong smells. For example, Matthew's favorite food is spicy chicken wings. I'm positive this is just to spite me.)

Another thing: Matty hated wearing clothes. My parents couldn't get him to keep them on. Of course, when we went out in public, he would be fully clothed. But the second we got home, he would rip off everything and cannonball into the nearest pile of snow. It's like his senses were so dull that a polar bear plunge was the only thing that could wake them up.

Right from the beginning, Matthew and I were different. He hadn't even been alive for a full year, and he could speak—a privilege I could not exploit until much, much later. Then, when he was around three years old, his speech slowly started to disappear. Eventually he stopped speaking entirely. Once I started talking, on the other hand, I just kept on going and have not shut up to this day. It was like we switched places, and from that point on, we continued to develop very differently.

As we grew older, we both acquired fixations—something common to many people on the spectrum. But even our fixations were polar opposites. Mine was watching movies, and his were eating and running. That meant our physiques developed very differently, too. Now, as a teenager, he has the body of an Olympian—six feet tall and two hundred pounds.

Even our approaches to life were at odds. I was a child who would overthink things—sometimes so deeply that I was unable to make a decision. I needed the approval of others to perform the smallest action. My brother, on the other hand, was driven purely by instinct. If he was hungry, he would grab an apple off a tree. If he was thirsty, he would jump in a lake and start drinking. His thought process was, "If I need a thing,

I'll go get the thing." I envied his drive, if not his questionable practicality.

As we got older, though, we found things we had in common. For one, he's got an incredible sense of humor. He and I are very similar in that we use humor to combat sadness. He likes to get a reaction and laughs when he knows he's getting it. His favorite thing to do is to abruptly change the radio station when you're listening to a song you like. Or smear peanut butter on door knobs. (That last one is not quite as endearing.)

One thing Matty taught me from early on was how accepting people could be of someone else's challenges and quirks. You might imagine that hanging around the house naked and diving into snowbanks would raise some eyebrows. But after the initial surprise, people were usually cool with it, whether it was neighbors, support workers, or friends who came over. They'd shrug. "That's just Matty being Matty." Having a supportive, nonjudgmental community around has always been a huge help for my family.

> **One thing Matty taught me from early on was how accepting people could be of someone else's challenges and quirks.**

Growing up with Matty helped shape the way I treat people, too. When you see someone naked in front of you—

emotionally or physically—you become very accepting of their vulnerability. It meant I was never afraid of seeing people at their low points. And I learned to work harder to understand people who didn't think the same way as me. That last lesson would prove useful as I got ready to face my biggest challenge yet: school.

Chapter 3

THE ELEMENTARY SCHOOL DOORSTOP

Not long after I had started school, the teacher asked our class a question:

"How many students are there at Mono-Amaranth Public School?"

I raised my hand and said, "There are three hundred and fifty-two students."

She looked surprised and asked how I knew.

In case you are assuming I must be on the end of the autism spectrum that gives you some savant-like ability to exactly calculate the size of crowds, that is not the case. The real reason I knew was because I had been taught that when you were going outside, it was polite to hold the door for the person after you. So, on my first day of school, when it was time for recess, I held the door for the student behind me.

And the next one. And the one after that. By the time I had counted all 351 of my schoolmates walking through the door, recess was over.

Nobody made eye contact.

Nobody said thank you.

When I got my diagnosis, my folks realized they were going to have to put in a little extra effort. They knew I was going to be different from other kids, that I might not be as socially savvy as my peers, and that they would have to teach me how to act like the others so as not to get ostracized.

I was taught how to "act normal." I learned to hold the door for people. I learned to tell the truth, but to understand when it was okay to lie for politeness. I learned to use my manners, not to swear, to respect personal space, and to stop talking when it was time for somebody else to have a turn.

And then I got to school. And I discovered that no one else had learned these things.

It was clear to me that the other parents—the ones with "normal" kids—hadn't taught their offspring basic etiquette, figuring they'd just pick it up on their own. If their kid didn't have a diagnosis, they obviously didn't think they needed to worry about it. And I felt cheated. Why did I have to learn how to be polite and respectful when other kids didn't?

Is Everyone a Little Bit Autistic?

Neurotypical. Autistic. They have things in common, but at the end of the day, you can't be "a little autistic," or, as I like to call it, "autist-ish." You either have autism or you don't, and while saying things like "Oh, I hate loud noises, too" might be meant to make people feel included, it also potentially trivializes a person's daily struggles.

There's a world of difference between having autistic tendencies and actually having autism. Like any neurological variation, autism borrows traits found in most of the neurotypical population. But everything a neurotypical feels, a person with autism feels at an 11. Still, while not everyone is autistic, it is good to notice the things we share in common so we can find ways to connect.

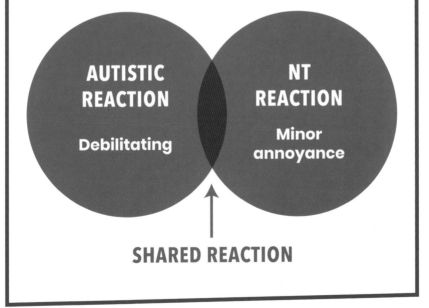

It's tough when you're a kid on the spectrum. Up until very recently—and even now, sometimes—there was a hazy understanding among the general population about what autism is. Even my own understanding at that age was a little muddled. For instance, when I was a kid, I thought my autism somehow tied into my lactose intolerance. Really, my folks had stopped giving me ice cream because it made me depressed for some reason. But somehow, those two completely unrelated things had formed a connection in my brain. So, for the longest time, when people asked me what autism was, I'd say, "It means I can't have milk."

My other default line was: "Can I take the cheese off that pizza? I can't eat it because of my autism."

Obviously, I wasn't the best autism educator as a kid. But in my line of work, I've been interviewed a few times, and I'm a little more prepared now for the question that will inevitably be asked: "What is autism?" Even still, it's a surprisingly hard question to answer.

The simplest definition is that autism is a neurological variation. In less fancy language, it's a difference in your brain and how it's wired. You see and process things differently from people who are the norm—what we in the ASD community call neurotypical.

Autism deals in extremes: you have a lot more of something and a lot less of something else. Imagine you're playing a game of Dungeons & Dragons where you have different attributes, like strength and dexterity. Now imagine you have 100 percent of one attribute and 15 percent of everything else. That's what being autistic can feel like: it's an imbalance. For instance, you might have a strong drive to act on your impulses, but less of the common sense that would help you control said impulses. Or you might have too much common sense, to the point where you can't take action because you're always thinking about what could go wrong. I've been both of these at different points in my life.

AUTISM Nutrition Facts

Serving Size - 1 person

	% Daily Value
Total Honesty	110%
Intentional	80%
Unintentional	30%
Introverted	75%
Logical	95%
Determined	100%
Focused	100%
Persistent	100%
Anxiety	85%
Underestimated	97%
Awesome	12397%

Non-Judgmental	100%	Obervant	90%
Eccentric	89%	Awkward	80%
Original	100%	Hidden Agendas	0%
Direct	100%	Ingenious	100%

Typical individuals with ASD don't attack the reputations of those around them; don't discriminate against anyone based on race, gender, age, or any other surface criteria; don't force others to live up to demanding hierarchies, and so are unlikely to give someone superior status simply because that person is wealthy or has attained a high position in an organization. They do have values that aren't shaped by financial, social, or political influences. They make very good employees when able to control their pace and work within either a solitary or socially supportive environment.

Daily values may vary by person depending on their disposition.

The Autism nutritional guide was created by and is the property of Michael McCreary - AspieComic. All rights reserved.

People sometimes use terms like "high-functioning" and "low-functioning" to describe folks on the spectrum, which can be wrongly taken to make assumptions about people's intelligence. Really, what they're meant to tell you is to what degree someone can get through their day independently, or how much assistance they might need in their daily lives.

There are a lot of other stereotypes about autism. For example, some people think being autistic means you're unable to perceive the thoughts and emotions of others.

Actually, based on my experiences and from talking to other people on the spectrum, it's quite the opposite: you feel every possible emotion and see every possible outcome of a social situation at once. It's kind of like being Doctor Manhattan from the comic *Watchmen*: you're seeing several time lines happening simultaneously. But unlike Doctor Manhattan, you can't teleport to Mars every time you feel overwhelmed, so you shut down and remove yourself socially. People are exhausting, and when your brain is working overtime to try to understand them, it can suck the joy out of socializing.

Having autism is like having too many tabs open on a computer. Or more accurately, it's like trying to surf the web without an ad blocker. Every time you click on something, another window pops up.

It should have been clear right away from the incident at recess, but over my first few years in school, it became more and more obvious that there was a distance between me and the other kids. Some of them called me Alfred—after the Batman character—because I was kind of like the school butler. I'd hold the door for people; I was always polite and well-spoken. I said sorry all the time, for everything, and I genuinely meant it. Coached by my parents, I developed a friendly, small-town manner.

Only that was the problem: friendly and polite had gone out of style. My constant apologizing came across as disingenuous to many kids, and in a world jaded by British TV murder mysteries, people can't help but think of "nice" as a tad sinister. For instance, in Toronto, where I live now, if you smile at someone on the street, they'll give you a funny look back, like, "What are you trying to sell me? Beat it, weirdo!"

Having autism is like having too many tabs open on a computer.

However, I didn't really realize any of this at the time. In fact, I thought I was doing quite well with people. In school, I was very open about my diagnosis. I told my classmates about my autism and tried to explain what it was. Of course, then they would go home and talk to their parents about it and come back with some misguided notions. To put it nicely, they figured I wasn't terribly perceptive. Somehow, they got it into their heads that they could do things to me and get away with it, and I wouldn't be any the wiser.

One of the difficult things about autism is that when you're talking to people, there can be a cognitive dissonance between the words they're saying and their body language. So, if someone is smiling at me while calling me a moron, I'll think they're a nice guy and they're just joking around. It wasn't always clear to me when someone was actually making fun of me, and I often didn't realize it until another person pointed it out.

One day in grade three, I was on the playground with another kid who was pelting me in the face with snowballs. I remember him saying, "It's okay! We're having a snowball fight!" as he threw more snow in my face. There was a lot wrong with this picture. For starters, this was not a fair fight. We were behind a skating rink in March and he was standing right next to the only pile of snow.

But then I saw my older brother, Andrew, come up behind the kid. Like a vengeful Elmer Fudd, he put his finger over his lips to indicate that I should be vawy, vawy quiet. He walked up to the guy, kicked him hard in the shin, and said, "Never talk to my brother again."

He didn't. I never saw that guy again. And Andrew gave me a warning: "Don't talk to him, or anyone like him. They're pretending to be nice, but they're not. Just because someone is smiling and saying nice things doesn't mean they're telling the truth."

It was good advice, but unfortunately, I didn't completely absorb it the first time. It would be a long—and painful—time before I learned how to recognize when I was being tricked. And an even longer time to figure out how to stand up for myself.

Chapter 4

BREAKING MY LEGS

What I've always loved about being on-stage is that you know for certain how people feel about you. When you're like me and your brain doesn't make it easy for you to tell whether someone is playing with you or making you the butt of their joke, it's enormously comforting to be in front of an audience, who will let you know pretty quickly whether they love or hate you. I was lucky to catch the performing bug early, and the stage quickly became a safe haven for me.

Unfortunately, I can't say my performance debut was all that auspicious. When I was six, my folks enrolled me in jazz and tap-dance lessons, where both my teachers and peers tolerated me as they prepared an elaborate *Chicago*-inspired routine while I pretended to be Optimus Prime in the corner.

Come to think of it, that dance program almost made me quit performing forever. Not because I hated dancing, but because on the night of our recital, one of the older kids told me my bright orange suspenders looked stupid. It may sound petty, but at the age of six, I had already acquired a performer's ego, which is kind of like a stained-glass painting: begging to be looked at, but incredibly fragile.

Rather than quitting then and there, I walked out on stage with my class. The music started, everyone struck a pose, and I sat in the middle with my arms crossed for eight minutes. My folks pulled me out of the program after that.

It was silly for me to respond the way I did. I had ruined the experience of performing for the people who loved it. (I also ruined for myself the color orange, which, to be fair, is the worst of the secondary colors.) And I gave someone else the satisfaction of winning a fight they didn't even know they had started. I could never let them win again. Any time I failed after that, I resolved to own it. Which was great, because I screwed up a lot.

Take my first play, *The Story of the Birth of Christ*. It was around Christmastime at the Bible chapel by my house, which made the play especially topical. I was cast as a shepherd, and another kid named Michael was cast as my sheep. I didn't have any lines, and my only stage direction was to lead my sheep through the arch, walk off stage left, and then do literally nothing. The bar was especially low, but because the average height of a McCreary is only five-foot-eight, I still managed to hit my face on it.

I led Michael the sheep not through the arch, but around it, and then, with a strange lack of affect, yelled, "Oh no! I didn't walk through the arch."

Unexpectedly, the crowd loved my blatant screwup, even the pastor. (I wasn't too worried about him, because his favorite movie was *Life of Brian.*) I had gotten a little taste of stardom, and I needed more stage time! Luckily, that year I received a Christmas miracle: a school play.

> **Any time I failed after that, I resolved to own it. Which was great, because I screwed up a lot.**

I can't remember the exact title, but it was a fable about the humbling of a bratty princess who has to live with some farmers after her castle gets robbed. I was cast as one of the farmers. According to the script, he's just called "Dad Farmer." This role was a little trickier than my last one, because instead of having no lines, now I had three. But I wasn't afraid of memorizing them, because I knew that the audience was made up mostly of parents, and if there's anything parents love, it's watching kids flub their lines.

Opening night arrived, and it was time for my big scene. The girl playing my wife delivered her line perfectly: "How's the harvest, hon?"

A beat of silence.

"I forgot my line," I said, and smirked.

The audience roared. *Hey, that felt pretty good*, I thought.

To her credit, my stage wife kept her composure through a forced smile. "Oh, honey, that's a strange thing to say! Seriously, what about the harvest?"

I had enough comic instinct to know that if I did the same thing again, they'd laugh even more.

"Sorry. Still don't know my line!" More laughter. The audience was in the palm of my hand. For those glorious forty-five seconds, time stopped and I was no longer in an elementary school, smiling sheepishly at my folks, yearning for their approval. I was a performer.

I walked away from that play with two new loves in my life: the thrill of performing, and the girl who played my wife. We'd gotten along fine before then, but once we were cast as husband and wife, I figured it was meant to be. This is how I thought all relationships started. You pretend to love each other, and after a while, you become so used to pretending that it becomes true. Come to think of it, that might not be totally inaccurate.

I was unable to get past the fact that a play is a thing where you pretend to be people you aren't and figured we should start going out. My proposal came in the form of an off-key cover of the Temptations' "Ain't Too Proud to Beg" in front of our whole class. She was too kind/mortified to say no.

If you're thinking that grade three is a little too early to start dating, you would be correct. It certainly wasn't on the minds of my classmates, who would always gag at the romantic parts in movies. But as a kid who didn't fully understand the spectrum of human emotions, I had trained myself with media to figure out how "normal" people acted. I always liked relationship movies and often would feel real heartache over them. And because I'd been raised on a diet of movies with twenty-somethings playing high school students asking each other, "When are you going to get a date?" I thought, *Well, I better get on that.* So, when I was the first in my class to get a date, at age ten, I was impressed with myself for making such good time.

I got my mom to chauffeur us to the fanciest joint in town: East Side Mario's. This was especially convenient because I had one of those "Dinner and a Movie" coupons. So we feasted on unlimited garlic bread and snuck what we couldn't finish into the theater for *Shrek the Third.*

I came to school the next day with a spring in my step. At the time, nothing could hurt me. Then, suddenly, everything did. My girlfriend dumped me. It turned out she had found out that I told everyone we were dating. Which, apparently, had been news to her.

There are two lessons here. Don't take your date to *Shrek the Third.*

And make sure you both know it's a date first.

Stereotypes

"Autism isn't real."
Correction: Stop reading the YouTube comments section.

"Autistic people hate being social and don't want relationships."
Correction: Autistic people want relationships, but on their own terms. Some prefer one-on-one interaction. Others like to keep it to a Skype call.

"Autistic people don't lie."
Correction: Autistic people are very honest in that they say what they're thinking. They're also capable of lying, usually to cover up something they don't want to do but can't find the words to explain why.

"People with autism are eccentric geniuses who love math and science."
Correction: I'm living proof of the opposite. I'm so bad at math, I'm the reason teachers started giving out participation ribbons at the end of math tests.

"People with autism have no sense of humor."
Correction: Rude! We do have a sense of humor, but a lot of jokes involve wordplay and sarcasm, which can be hard for the literal-minded. Or maybe the joke just wasn't that funny.

Things weren't looking much brighter on the acting front. After my moment of flubbed-line stardom, I was eager to star in a new play. So, I asked my teacher, "What's our next production?" As it turned out, my school didn't have one planned for the foreseeable future.

That simply could not be. I decided I would write a play myself. That very night, I went home and started dictating the script to my dad. I wanted to create a play, a masterful play that would inspire countless generations of Orangevillians hereafter. I imagined the town erecting a statue in my honor in the *middle of the road.*[*]

I was determined to write a towering masterpiece of the theater for my grade three class. *The SpongeBob SquarePants Movie* had just come out, and I had found my muse. For whatever reason, I became obsessed with a minor character called Dennis, an Alec Baldwin–voiced fish bounty hunter sent to kill SpongeBob and Patrick by the villainous Plankton. I felt it was a major injustice that Dennis wasn't the main character of *The SpongeBob SquarePants Movie*. And so was birthed *The SpongeBob SquarePants Movie: The Play.*

There were a lot of logistical details to work out. First, I had to convince my teacher to let me put on my play. Luckily, I had

---

[*] For context, Orangeville has a statue in the middle of the road because the town wanted to create a tourist trap, since there was no other way to get people to stop in Orangeville. They stuck in a reservoir, a clock tower, and a statue of Sir Orange Lawrence, the town founder, right in the center of the street. Great for sightseers. Bad for ambulances.

a very special teacher. She had already worked with me for two years by this point, and she recognized the challenges I had, especially with things like math and science. Not only was she deeply empathetic, but she always challenged me to work around problems and find new learning strategies. I think she recognized that this play could be a breakthrough for me. It was the beginning of someone who wanted to create, and she chose to foster that quality in me. I'll always be grateful to her for that.

More Stereotypes

"Women can't be autistic."

Correction: This is a fallacy. Many females on the spectrum go undiagnosed for prolonged periods of time because autism presents differently in women and men. This lower rate of diagnosis is in part due to the neurological model used by most doctors being a male one.

"Autistic people are incapable of feeling emotion."

Correction: Look, we're not Vulcans. I've said it before, and I'll say it again. Our society's conception of empathy is misleading. Just because you don't show what you're feeling, doesn't mean you aren't feeling something. Also, I definitely cried at the end of *The Wrath of Khan*.

"People with autism are really, really good looking."

Correction: Nope, this is pretty spot-on.

The next step was to get my classmates on board and cast them in the appropriate roles. Every night I'd go home and dictate the play to my dad, who wrote it all down in pen, and every day I'd go to class and try to gauge the level of enthusiasm from my classmates. One kid thought it was a dumb idea, so I gave him the part of Phil, who had one line: "Oh no." The kids who were moderately interested got around ten lines each. If they seemed really ambitious, they'd get twenty-five lines.

I was playing Dennis, of course, and I was confident I could carry the play. But I knew that Dennis couldn't have the most lines, because it would be misleading for him to have more lines than the titular character, SpongeBob. While Dennis was obviously the best character, a more mainstream audience might not see things the same way I did. So I put aside my auteurist vision in favor of a compromise. I counted very carefully so that SpongeBob had 157 lines, whereas Dennis had only 156. Dennis was also in every scene except the first one.

The hardest challenge was to cast an actor to play SpongeBob. I had two classmates who wanted the part, but I wasn't sure if either of them could memorize all 157 lines. So I split the play into two acts and decided that one actor would play SpongeBob for the first half, and then in act two, the second actor would take over. The audience would have to suspend a little disbelief as to how SpongeBob suddenly got a foot taller in the second act, but so what?

My folks went all in for me in this project. Not only did my dad serve as stenographer, but my mom made costumes for the whole cast. Extra kudos has to go to my teacher. It's not every teacher who would let their student put on a forty-five-minute piece of theatrical fan fiction about a cartoon sponge.

After one cold read and one dress rehearsal, performance day finally arrived. My classmates were bubbling with enthusiasm in their costumes. I set up a mini boom box in the corner of the classroom to play bits of the movie soundtrack as scenic interludes. And the audience—consisting of the teacher, and my parents with a video camera—waited excitedly for the show to begin.

The first act went great. It didn't even matter that my classmates had their scripts in hand. (It turned out memorizing lines wasn't so easy for third-graders.) As the only actor off book, I managed to find a way to ad lib, even in a play I had written myself.

At the climax of the play, my character, Dennis, was vanquished by SpongeBob and Patrick, and I was lying on the floor incapacitated. SpongeBob sang the climactic song, which was a parody of the Twisted Sister 1980s hair-metal anthem "I Wanna Rock." Only the second-act SpongeBob didn't know the lyrics—something I found especially annoying as he was holding the script I gave him with the lyrics written down. In my frustration, I jumped up, rushed to the front, and began belting out the song, which was a bit puzzling to everyone because I was supposed to be dead. So much for continuity.

In spite of my megalomaniac tendencies, the play was a hit. My parents were beaming with pride, and I felt like I was walking on clouds. I had created something and shared it with other people, and it was an amazing feeling. Later that year I even won a school award for it, in the "effort" category.

Unfortunately, this is one of the great plays lost to the ages. My parents still have the performance recorded on video, but whoever had used the camera before me had it set to the night-vision setting, which means all the colors are inverted. So that's how I accidentally created an art film in grade three.

Having now written and starred in my own play, I wanted to stretch my wings beyond the confines of school theater. I started acting in Theatre Orangeville's Young Company, which was run by a brilliant director named Jane Cameron. She ran an eclectic program, with a mix of typical kids' plays like *Alice in Wonderland* alongside experimental plays, written by Jane herself, which were very sophisticated deconstructions of the typical kid-show formula. She was great at making sure that every person in the play got the same number of lines and would work one on one with the actors to help them hone their craft. She was a great mentor and an even better friend.

But inevitably, in a youth production, there comes this scene. It's usually near the end of the second act, following a major plot twist. The whole cast gathers onstage in a semi-circle and each cast member says one line, in sequence. This scene is awful. One, because it's in every kids' play ever. And two, because someone always forgets their line. You can't mask this mistake by walking around and riffing with the crowd; you just have to sit there for a small eternity while whoever forgot their line gets their act together. And that's in a scenario where only one person forgets their line!

I was still harboring some lingering frustration with my classmate for not knowing his song lyrics in my SpongeBob play. Now, community theater was only exacerbating that frustration. It drove me crazy that I had to count on people to remember their lines, and when they would screw them up, there was nothing I could do to fix it.

I loved acting, but I was starting to realize that maybe group work just wasn't for me. I never got the hang of depending on other actors. So I resolved to explore more independent creative avenues. Ones that would grant me more control. I came up with two options, and they both had to do with the California Raisins.

For those of you too young to remember, the California Raisins were a group of Motown-singing Claymation characters created by a marketing board in the 1980s to sell shriveled fruit. They starred in commercials, TV specials, and their own line of toys and accessories. They were huge. You had to be there. You could say it was my latest in a long line of past and future fixations.

A fixation is, at its essence, just a love of something. Most people have hobbies or passions. But for people with autism, their fixation is the driving force behind everything they do. It might be pro wrestling, World War I aviation, insects, or Kodak cameras—anything we can research, systematize, and organize is comfortable for us. The downside: if you ask an Aspie, "Hey, what are you into?" be prepared to lose several hours.

> **If you ask an Aspie, "Hey, what are you into?" be prepared to lose several hours.**

So, some people had the Beatles, others had the Rolling Stones. I had the Raisins. I watched their *Behind the Music* tape until my VCR exploded. I realized then and there that I had to choose between my two new loves: the power of song, or the magic of stop-motion animation. It took about two tubes of Play-Doh, a disposable camera, and twenty minutes on a muggy April morning to realize that maybe I should stick to singing Stevie Wonder covers.

I was off to the talent show sign-up sheet. I wrote my name down in all-caps and replaced the L in "Michael" with an exclamation mark, because I thought that was cool. Then again, I also thought the California Raisins were cool, so I might not have been the best judge.

At my school, we ran our talent show a little differently. It was called MAPS IDOL (MAPS stood for Mono-Amaranth Public School), a school-friendly knockoff of the then-popular series *American Idol*. We even had a panel of judges comprised of the high school improv team, who all wanted to be the very British and very rude Simon Cowell. This was especially fun because they were forbidden from being mean like Simon, so instead they responded to each performance with: "Jolly good."

I went up there and sang the only song I knew, "Ain't Too Proud to Beg." My (sort of) ex-girlfriend didn't like that too much, but the crowd didn't seem to mind. As a matter of fact, I even won the Students' Choice Award! Which was impressive, given that I only hit every other note.

Chapter 5

THE FUNISHER: VOL. 1

Unfortunately, the incident with the snowballs in grade three wasn't a one-time thing. Some kids just seemed to sense my difficulty in interpreting social cues and would take advantage of me. And the saddest thing was, I never had a clue.

For instance, when I was in the young acting company, there was another actor I would regularly joke around with. I thought we were getting along great. Until one day he was pulled aside by one of the older actors who had been watching us, who told him sternly, "Don't talk to Michael like that ever again." My "friend" had been making fun of me, but because he was smiling the whole time, I hadn't even realized it.

I was devastated. *Why am I getting picked on in youth theater?* I asked myself. *We're all nerds!*

But it happened again, this time at my cousin's house.

Again, I thought we were having a good time. My cousin and I had been at odds before, but I thought he had really come around. Nope. Only twenty minutes into a game of "Michael Closes His Eyes and Counts Forever While We Leave to Play Mario Kart," my uncle pulled him aside and said, "How dare you treat your cousin like that?"

I almost would have preferred not to find out. *Oh, just let me dream!* I thought. *Let me live the lie!* It was always a heartbreaking thing to learn secondhand that people—people who I thought liked me—were actually messing with my mind. And as time went on, it started to really put me at odds with others. I wasn't sure who I could trust.

By grade six, this sort of thing had been happening long enough that I didn't need it pointed out to me anymore. I started to recognize when other people were messing with me. The second my friends—or the people I thought were my friends—started exhibiting those behaviors toward me, I alienated myself from the group. And gradually, I removed myself from every social situation because I couldn't trust people. Frankly, I hated people. So I became a loner. I disappeared into the background.

And then in grade seven, something changed.

Other kids with ASD started coming to my school. I saw that people were treating them the same way they treated me. And I said to myself, *This is it. I'm going to stand up for my people. This is my destiny, to be the hero that the autism community needs.*

I was very self-righteous. Also, there were only four of us; it wasn't much of a community.

I became a sort of autistic vigilante. At this point I want to issue a disclaimer. I do not condone any of my actions described here. Do NOT do what I did. Even if it was totally awesome.

To put it in context, my school wasn't exactly the poster school for sensitive and thoughtful behavior. Not only were the autistic youth bullied, but so were other kids for various sexist, racist, or ableist reasons. For example, one of my classmates went as a Chinese person for Halloween. He was not Chinese. While teachers tried to quell this kind of behavior to the best of their ability, there was only so much they could do. The hallways and playgrounds were populated with a variety of petty racists and Pixy Stix–snorting goons.

But Harold was a bully in a league all his own. For one thing, he was the most popular guy in school. He was charismatic, great at sports, a good student—this guy excelled at everything he did. And everyone thought he was cool. Even the parents loved him. My mom went to a PTA meeting once and they spent half the time talking about how wonderful Harold was.

But I rode the bus home every day with Harold, and I knew the truth. Because Harold wasn't the kind of bully who would come up to your face and insult you. He was much too cool for that. He had more of a creepy Hannibal style of bullying: he didn't eat people, but he was good at getting under people's skin. Every day he would hold court on the bus and say horrible things about every person in our class.

Small Talk Mad Libs

Almost everything I do is scripted, right down to my social interactions. My folks spent countless hours teaching me how to act natural. The tough part is, life isn't scripted, and after the initial "How do you do," I'd usually panic. To save the next generation of autistic folk from such embarrassment, I've developed a script of sorts to help them out.

_____ , how are you? Oh, and how are/is the _____?
(pleasant greeting)   *(inoffensive noun)*

I couldn't help but notice your _____ . It looks great.
                                        (ugliest thing in sight)

How about that _____? Anyways, I really should be
                        (inane subject)

_____ . You know how _____ is.
    (plausible excuse to leave)   *(easily relatable work thingy)*

I'd love to pick this up _____ .
                                (much, much later; keep room for prep time)

Perhaps we could _____ .
                        (a social outing that is broad enough to appease anyone, but
                        specific enough to show you both have something in common)

Before I go, could I get your _____ .
                                (contact info that you might already have)

Oh, wait! We didn't do our _____ .
                                (inexplicable secret handshake)

Yeah, now's probably not the time. Well enjoy your _____ .
                                                    (pick a time of day)

_____ !
(monosyllabic word confirming that you're leaving forever now)

One day one of his underlings gave him a letter from a girl who liked him. He just smirked and ripped it up in front of everyone. He made fun of kids with special needs. And he loved to pit people against each other. He was like the lord in his castle, making catty comments and watching the proletariat masses below fight it out.

The first time I ever thought the word "douche," it was because of him. It just formed it my head, like an exploding neon sign. I didn't even know the word before that point, but it seemed to fit.

"How can someone who's so good at things be so mean to people?" I would often ask. "What does he have to be mean about?"

I decided I had to do something. I would expose Harold for the hypocrite he was. Every day I planned my strategy as I watched him on the bus, conning and sweet-talking people. He had them all in the palm of his hand.

"Not for long, you sonofabitch," I actually muttered to myself.

I went home and got creative. It was just before Christmas, so I thought the mischief-making of *Home Alone* would be a fine point of reference. The next day was the last day of school before the winter break, and I knew what I was going to do.

The next day, after the last class had ended, everyone was saying their goodbyes for the holidays. My parents were picking me up and they were five minutes late, which was perfect. I had just enough time. I took a banana I had brought for lunch and put it in a plastic bag. I poked a couple of holes in it and put it in Harold's desk, so that over the course of two weeks, it would rot and completely consume his desk.

The holidays passed, and in January, we all came back to school. Everyone was dragging themselves back into the routine, complaining about how much they hated school, and so on. Not Harold. He was all tanned and cocky, probably having spent the winter skiing in Kelowna. He sat down smugly at his desk.

And now we come to the single greatest moment of my life.

"Open your books to page forty-three," said the teacher. "We're going to talk about the War of 1812."

But Harold wasn't prepared for war. Not this one.

He opened the top of his desk. From where I was sitting, I couldn't see what it looked like. But I could put together a fairly good image from what he screamed:

"WHO SHIT IN MY DESK?"

Silence in the classroom. Then laughter.

I grinned. No one knew it was me. Or so I thought.

After that incident, Harold didn't seem quite so keen on bad-mouthing people. Maybe I really had made a difference. I congratulated myself for my brilliantly sneaky tactics.

But two months later, Harold somehow got wind that I was the one who had planted the banana, and he confronted me.

"I know what you did," he said. "Why do you hate me?"

Smile!

While I was polite as a kid, I wasn't terribly emotive. One thing I get asked a lot that I'm sure many autistic people can relate to is: "Smile! What's wrong with you?" Ironically, one of the only times I got into trouble in elementary school was because I smiled.

For context, I was playing soccer in gym class. And by playing, I mean I was watching the three resident jocks (all named Luke) hog the ball for ninety minutes. The teacher didn't like that most of us were standing around and decided to make us wait in the corner until the Lukes finished their game. I thought this was a perfect time to practice my smile so that it would get my classmates off my back about never smiling. But I guess it wasn't, because when the teacher saw me doing this, she screeched: "What are you smiling about?!" In truth, nothing.

ANGRY

HAPPY

NERVOUS

EXCITED

GASSY

FLIRTY

This was it. The moment I'd been prepping for.

I asked him, "How much time do you have?"

I've mentioned that people on the autism spectrum tend to become fixated on things. Well, my fixation at this particular point in time was ruining Harold's life. So I laid out all of his faults. I told him, "Everyone is so nice to you. You're the captain of the team, the best player at every sport, you win at everything. Everyone wants to be you. And you're horrible. To everyone. I don't think you deserve the friends you have. That's why I hate you."

"Oh," he said.

If I could have marched away triumphantly after that, it would have been great. But unfortunately, it was the middle of the day, between classes. Harold and I both had to go French class next and we were in the same group. So we just had to sit together awkwardly for a while.

I couldn't sleep at night for a week afterward, wondering how he had found out about the banana. After all, we had never actually spoken before he confronted me; I merely hated him from a distance. It turned out that someone had seen me lingering in the school before winter break, and he had sold me out. The irony was that he was one of the guys who Harold had been actively abusing and someone I thought I had been sticking up for. People made fun of this kid because he would suddenly blurt things out loud. Other people thought he was weird, but I could tell there was something wrong with his wiring. (He was later diagnosed with Tourette's syndrome.) So

I thought I was defending this guy with my banana vigilantism. Only he told on me to Harold because he wanted to be accepted and liked by the in-group.

That really shined a light on my own narcissism. I had thought I would be given a medal, celebrated as a hero for taking down the bully. But everyone else's life went on, and they had to still function within the system. It might have made me feel good in the moment, but these kids were still getting bullied.

So that started a shift in my thinking. Maybe pranking these guys wasn't the best way. I had learned how to stand up for myself, or what I thought was standing up for myself. But what would take me a little longer to learn was how to seek out justice without hurting others.

That said, in the days and weeks that followed, it really seemed like Harold had taken my words to heart and realized that he should stop treating people badly.

Selfishly, I didn't want him to. In Harold, I'd finally found my nemesis. One that I could always count on to do bad, so that I could always be there to do good. Locked in an eternal battle of wits. But life isn't like a superhero movie. Harold had an incredibly mature response to my criticism, and he actually grew and changed as a human being.

So I decided I would try to grow and change, too. The next time I saw another bully making fun of a special needs girl,

I thought I would try a different tactic. Instead of scolding him, I simply explained her situation to him, as clearly and straightforwardly as I could. He didn't say anything, but he looked thoughtful. Not long after, I actually saw him playing with her.

I figured out that people don't usually change if you put bananas in their desks. When they change is if you help them see the other as a human being.

With my vigilante instincts fading, I started to channel my energy into advocating for myself and other kids on the spectrum in a more positive way. I saw the perfect opportunity to practice when I was confronted with the burning injustice of gym class dodgeball practice.

It had been happening for years. The captains would choose teams in each class. The same four jocks would get picked first, and the ASD kids in the special ed class would get picked last. I saw how demoralizing it was to all of us and how it made kids feel even more alone than they already did. So I decided I would have a talk with my gym teacher and explain why this was a problem. She listened and told me that for the next class, I would be the captain in charge of picking one team, and another kid from special ed would be the other captain. Finally, a chance to overturn the years of jock supremacy!

I dutifully made my first pick: one of the kids from the ASD class. He ran up to me, and I could see the amazement on his face and the tears in his eyes. He said, "Oh my God. Thank you! That's the first time anyone's ever picked me for anything." It was a really beautiful, heartfelt moment between us.

> **I figured out that people don't usually change if you put bananas in their desks.**

One by one, I picked all the other ASD kids in the class for my team, only to see the surprise and joy reflected on their faces as well. I felt proud, like I was leading my people into battle.

The other captain, also on the spectrum, took a different approach. He picked all the best athletes in the class. You know, the kind of guys who drink meat shakes for lunch. It was a massacre. Halfway through the game, the guy I picked first, who had been so grateful to me, screamed, "Why did you pick me?!"

What can I say—I tried.

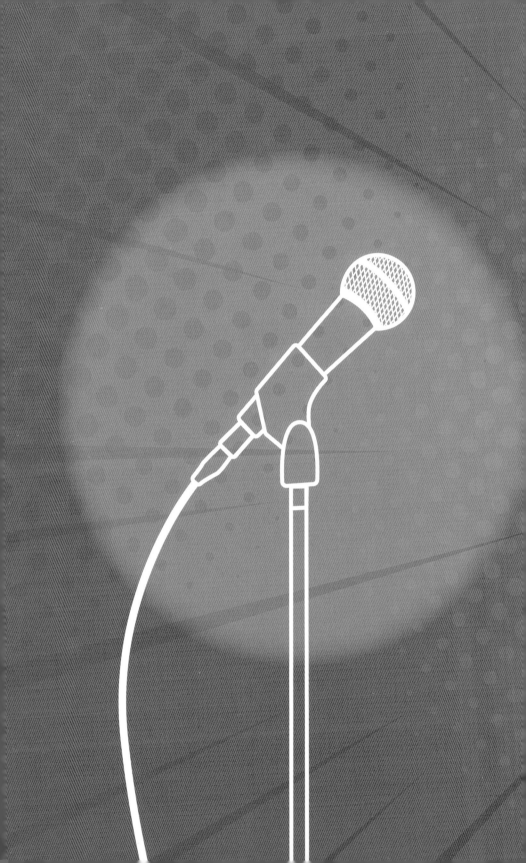

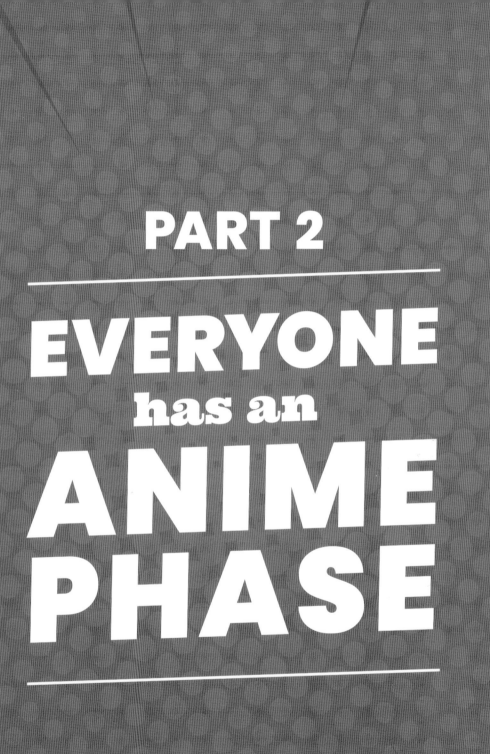

PART 2

EVERYONE has an ANIME PHASE

No one likes being a teenager.

No one likes you when you're a teenager. But, luckily for all of us, it only lasts seven years. And for me, and probably for most other people with ASD, it's an awkward stretch of time we'd much rather forget. (Please note the title above.) We're even more awkward than the average gawky teen. The constantly shifting social cues of teenage life are even more confusing for us to navigate. School and its expectations can be especially hard on many with ASD, and the quest to fit in can be even trickier when you're already marked as different.

At the same time, our teenage years are when many of us start to figure out who we are, find a tribe we can belong to, and discover the passions that will carry us through life.

Let me regale you with tales of a time not long ago (the early 2010s) in a place far, far away (Southern Ontario). A time of soul-searching that led me to discover stand-up comedy and desperate attempts to reinvent myself in the dystopian teenage wasteland we call high school.

Chapter 6

MICHAEL BEGINS: THE SEARCH FOR APPROVAL

When I was in grade seven, my mom introduced me to journaling. This was partly a solution to a long-standing problem. Ever since I was a little kid, I would come home from school and my mom would ask how my day went.

"Well, at 9:00 a.m. the bell went and at 9:01 we sang 'O Canada' and at 9:04 we sat down and got out our books ...," I would reply. And so on, and on.

So buying me a journal was the politest way she could figure out to shut me up. And it worked out great for both of us. It allowed me to vent about my day, and it let her cherish twelve extra minutes of silence each night before I inevitably started talking again.

As my adolescent rage grew, fueled by the bullying I was enduring at school, my entries began to change. At first, I thought I was pouring out my soul. Exorcising some real demons. When I actually read back what I had written, though, something unexpected happened—it made me laugh. *Maybe I'm actually writing jokes*, I thought. I started to refine and shape my material. Soon I had pages and pages full of jokes.

I started to test my new material out on my folks. Each night at dinner, I'd read them what I had written. We had a pretty good system worked out. I'd tell a few jokes, and they'd be brutally honest. They were tough but fair critics.

"If people think rain is God peeing," I would begin my routine between bites of dinner, "what do they think he's doing when it snows?"

"Inappropriate," my dad would say. He's the stern one, an old soul who grew up in the 1950s, though beneath the conservative exterior, he's a bleeding-heart liberal who cries at every movie he sees, even the bad ones.

"You need to fucking eat," my mom would chime in. She's the free spirit, a warm humanist with a crass sense of humor and the wonderful ability to see people as complicated and accept them in spite of their flaws.

At times like that I would think about how much of a perfect synthesis of my parents I am and how much each of them has contributed to my strengths and vulnerabilities as a person and a comedian. From my dad—a businessman and natural leader, who's organized more fundraisers for autism than

I can count—I got my stage presence and micromanaging neuroses. From my mom I got my empathy, compassion, and crippling fear of disapproval. Shake well and you get one stand-up comic. Now all I needed were some better jokes.

My comedy routines might not have always killed it at the dinner table, but my parents could see that this was something I loved to do, and they wanted to encourage me. My mom suggested that I enrol in a program she had stumbled upon in the local paper. David Granirer, a Vancouver-based comedian known as the Happy Neurotic, was running a series of stand-up comedy workshops just outside of my town. David had built a career around using his own mental illness in comedy, and the program, called Stand Up For Mental Health, had the mission of using stand-up to eliminate the stigma around both psychological and neurological variations.

I loved that sentiment. And I think it might have landed better if those classes hadn't been held at an out-of-use hospital on top of a hill next to a graveyard. There was lightning on the night I first showed up. I'm not making any of this up. But at least there were Oreos once you got inside!

The atmosphere didn't help my nerves. And as soon as I walked in, I was caught off guard by how different I was from the rest of the group. For one thing, I was the youngest person there by far. I was thirteen years old, and everyone else was in their thirties and forties. As we began going around the room and introducing ourselves, I felt even more out of place. Here I was, a grade seven kid complaining about school bullies and pet peeves. And here were these adults with real, severe challenges. Some of them were agoraphobics and hadn't gone outside in three and a half years. Some had been in psych wards for a decade. This class was much-needed therapy, in every sense of the word, for them. I felt as though my problems were childish and not really legit. Maybe it was wrong that I was there. After all, I had a level of privilege these people had never experienced.

But if those fears were in my head, no one else seemed to see things that way. David did such an excellent job of making everyone feel at home, even though he wasn't there physically and was being projected onto a giant screen from Vancouver via Skype. He made his presence felt and made us feel that we all deserved to be there and our relative levels of privilege and suffering didn't matter: we all had our challenges, and the purpose of the workshop was to tear down the stigma around all of them.

And the rest of the group were incredibly accepting of the kid in their midst and wanted to make me feel welcome. They took me seriously and listened to me talk about my problems, never making me feel like I didn't deserve to be there. In fact, the gang even related to my struggles at the time, because, as I soon found out, they were pretty universal struggles. Everyone's been bullied. Everyone's felt like an outcast. This made me feel less alone.

After the intros, David asked me to volunteer to create the first joke. I stood up in the middle of the room.

"What's your diagnosis?" he asked me.

"Autism spectrum disorder," I replied.

"And what does that entail?" he asked.

I explained. "Well, I get fixated on niche subjects and talk too much about them."

"Does this get you in trouble?"

"Yes."

"Where?"

"At Bible camp," I replied. That got a laugh.

Then he taught me how to take that little kernel of my experience and construct a joke out of it.

Here's what I ended up with:

"I was talking to this guy. I thought we really connected. I told him everything, then suddenly he snapped at me. I was so embarrassed and didn't know what to do. So I left the confessional."

That was the first joke I ever wrote.

> ### Everyone's been bullied.
> ### Everyone's felt like an outcast.
> ### This made me feel less alone.

David taught me so much more, from how to construct a joke to how to work a crowd to always punching up—meaning you make jokes about the people in power, not the people without it.

At the end of the first night, David assigned us one piece of homework: go home and write two minutes' worth of material. The rest of the class did just that. I came back with ten minutes. It was cheating a little, because a lot of it was material from my journal, but I now knew how to punch it up and make it performance ready.

Info Dumping

Many Aspies dislike what most people think of as a normal conversation, where you say one sentence, then I'll say one, and we repeat that forever. I can never get out what I want to say in only one sentence—it usually takes me a few minutes.

But sometimes, you just can't listen to a fifteen-minute monologue about stamps or World War II fighter jets. And someone with autism might not pick up on the typical cues of boredom or frustration, like sighing or looking away. So if you get stuck in an info dump with an Aspie and they're not picking up on your hints, here are some tips:

1. Try to relate their story back to your own personal experience.

2. Be blunt about your needs. Blunt, not rude. Be kind and state what you want out of this conversation.

3. If you have to leave, let us know how much air time you have left. Even if you'll be leaving 20 seconds from now, we appreciate the mental prep time.

4. Interrupt between breaths. Everybody has to breathe sometime.

Winter turned to spring. I kept going to class, writing more material, and refining my jokes with the help of David and the group. And then, we booked our first show. It was at a university on the outskirts of Hamilton, Ontario, and our audience was made up entirely of professors. David flew out to perform with us in person. Because I had amassed the most material— now twelve minutes—David picked me to headline the show.

I was terrified. I was terrified because I knew that this was something I loved, and if I bombed on my first time out, I might never want to do it again. I was still only thirteen, and I felt like my whole future was on the line.

I spent the entire show in the green room nibbling on a jalapeño cheese ball. There were about ten comics in the lineup, which averaged about five minutes per comic, which equaled to me eating one entire jalapeño cheese ball. Then David called my name and I headed for the stage.

When I'd seen comics lean on a mic stand, I always thought it was a power move. I soon realized that it was meant to make your shaking look less obvious. Nothing in my life has scared me more than the first time I ever told a joke. Telling the joke itself is fine. You know all the words and the places to pause. What you don't know is whether or not people will laugh. And it's that beat of silence between the joke and the potential laughter that still shakes me to my core.

I did get a laugh, though. My first joke hit. And sure enough, so did the next one. And the next one. I flubbed the one after, but played it off like nothing. Twelve minutes went by, and I didn't want to get off the stage. But alas, it was a school night, and the professors needed to get home before dark. David brought all the comics back onstage for a bow, and all I could think about was, "When are we doing this again?" I knew that not every show could be as good as this one. But I had to keep doing them.

Chapter 7

I FOUGHT THE LAW, AND THE LAW CALLED MY PARENTS

My comedy career was off to a promising start. Unfortunately, I had to get through a little thing called "high school" before it could really take off.

I went into high school more than a little disillusioned. I figured that functionally, it was only a stepping stone to get into a college or a university, and yet I'd already decided that I didn't want to go to post-secondary school at all. On a muggy recess in June, I had grilled my grade seven teacher on the merits of a post-secondary education, and he couldn't give me a convincing answer. Frankly, he didn't give me any answer. When I asked him, "Can more school guarantee a job?" he pretended to go break up an imaginary fight.

A degree can be an incredible stepping stone. But by that point, I knew I wanted to be a stand-up comedian, and I didn't need a degree for that. By grade ten, I was already doing it— performing once a month and getting better and better. I was learning from older comics, going to comedy shows and workshops, and writing all the time.

My attitude is that school is what you make of it. It should be a place for you to sharpen your tools, to immerse yourself in a topic so deeply that you emerge ready for what comes next. Only school enforces a jack-of-all-trades mentality. Most people on the spectrum—and really, people in general—just aren't good at every subject. Instead of letting you spend time doing what you're great at, the structure of school usually means you have to spend more time on what you're not good at. For me, my English grades were fantastic, but I sucked at math, so I needed to do more math to get my grades up.

So high school, for me, was less about navigating the heady world of education to make something of myself and more of an opportunity to rebuild my social life and connect with some other lost souls on the angst-ridden, apocalyptic battlefield of high school.

My first year of high school did teach me one valuable lesson, though, and it was what a difference a good, responsive teacher can make to kids with special needs—and how much harder it is when the adults at school don't put in the effort to address your specific challenges. I learned this through my own experiences, as well as those of my brother Matthew.

My little brother came out of 2010 a changed person. He'd entered his grade eight year leading the school in violent incident reports and left … much less so. A lot of the progress could be chalked up to his teacher, Jeff (or as my folks called him, Saint Jeff), a man who was intuitive, empathetic, and wouldn't tolerate fools.

My folks had had a bad track record with the teachers in Matthew's special ed class over the years. Many of them couldn't think of a way to work around his erratic behavior and would instead opt to send him home. Educational assistants would get frustrated with his lack of compliance and stop doing their jobs. Jeff had no patience for any of this. He put his foot down and told the EAs, "I want each of you to tell me what you would do best with each of these students. You're all paid the same, you have the same training, and you're all going to work equally with each of these students. If that's a problem, transfer forms are in the office."

Some of them left.

Those who stayed, though, got to witness Matthew's transformation as Jeff implemented clever tools to make him feel less like an outsider. Rather than putting my brother in a separate room, Jeff installed a glass wall with a door in it at the back of the main classroom. This way Matty could learn with the rest of the class while not getting so excited as to slap someone. Once he was calmed down, he could participate with the group.

That year, he won the school Perseverance Award, the same one I won for writing my *SpongeBob SquarePants* fan-fic play all those years ago. I'd never been prouder of him.

In terms of my social position, I approached high school as a land of opportunity. I was coming from a measly student body of 352 into a much larger school with over a thousand students. Not to mention that there was a much larger group of autistic kids. In my elementary school, there had only been a handful of us on the spectrum, but in my high school, there were around thirty. So I felt I could more easily disappear and not have to stick out the way I did before.

But alas, I am a performer. Not to mention, my vigilante impulses were starting to come back in an unexpected way.

I made it through the first semester without making a scene. Mostly. My assigned locker had been taken over by a six-foot-tall goon who said it fell under the "Finders Keepers" rule. Because I still had the locker combination, I stuck a banana in it after school.

I had four classes a day: English, math, drama, and one I had never heard of before, called "learning strategies." This class was mandatory for the autistic students. It was meant to teach us how to assimilate. We mostly performed what they called "Getting to Know You" exercises, which I excelled in because I had gone to elementary school with almost a third of the class.

I couldn't help but be awed by the larger autistic student body. I had never been around such a variety of kids with autism, and I was amazed at all the different ways they approached their own diagnosis. One guy saw his autism as a source of shame and would come in late every day so that none of the neurotypicals in the hall could tell he was part of the class. Another guy would use his autism to excuse his bad behavior. And then there were people like me. Empathetic to our fellow students for feeling like outsiders. Empathetic to the teacher for trying his darndest to make the class feel like it mattered. Counting the seconds on the clock till we could leave.

Despite our at-times-contradictory views, we bonded. We started going off script from the usual "How Are You Today?" social story and got down to talking about what really mattered: nerd stuff. Mostly deconstructions of superhero movies. The class really lightened up after that, and we started to hang out as a group together outside of class, too, though it wasn't planned. It turned out that the whole Learning Strategies class had signed up for Anime Club, because, well, we're autistic. And because only autistic people watch anime, we ended holding our sessions in the special ed room, which we dubbed "the Hub."

The Hub was like an autistic Batcave. It had the best model train sets, the worst 1990s anime, and the most passive-aggressive educational assistants. It had everything!

Now, I don't hate EAs, but throughout my high school career, I observed many bad ones who would use what limited authority they had to make autistic students feel small. Let me give you an example. One day, my friend and I were the only ones in the Hub for lunch. We were talking about why the movie *Flyboys* sucked, him from a technical standpoint, me from a James Franco standpoint. Suddenly we heard a voice from across the room squawk, "You're being too loud!" Not ones for confrontation, we apologized and continued our conversation in a whisper.

My friend barely got a sentence out before the EA gave us an ultimatum: "Keep it down, or take it outside."

My friend went ballistic. He was crying, flapping his hands, and asking the obvious question: "If you have a problem with noise, why don't *you* go outside?" I said nothing. I'd never seen him get worked up like this, but I was too scared to help, even though I knew he was right to be mad.

I had no tolerance for that kind of behavior. We hadn't been bothering anyone. It seemed like a pointless exercise in authority, meant only to make us feel powerless. One week later, that same EA popped into the Hub for a cup of coffee. This particular pot had been brewed by my friend. The EA took one sip and made a scrunchy face. "Who made this?"

"I did," my friend muttered.

"It needs some work," the EA chirped.

For once in my life, I had the right thing to say for the situation. I swiveled around in my chair and hollered, "You have high standards for a guy who gets his coffee from the spec ed class!"

It was in this moment that I realized my quarrel would no longer be with schoolyard bullies; it would be with actual adults. And this war could not be fought with bananas.

The battle reached its apex in geography class. Applied geography. No one wanted to be there, least of all my friend Joseph, who was constantly bullied while our teacher actively ignored it. The three bullies in question, Zack, Chad, and Emilio, weren't exceptionally good bullies. At their worst, they were obnoxious, but never actively hostile. Mostly, they'd just say Joseph's name in a weird way and try to get him to snort chalk dust.

One day, Joseph finally gave in and did it. Afterward, he was begging for them to leave him alone. I was heartbroken. I suddenly saw a lot of myself in Joseph. I wasn't sure if he was autistic or not, but he just wanted to be liked and struggled to infer the motives of those who preyed on him, because they were smiling. It was way too familiar.

A few days later, when one of the bullies kept closing Joseph's laptop on him, I snapped. I exploded on the guy and told him to cut it out. He responded in a strange way that was simultaneously insane and yet totally appropriate for the situation. He frowned, nodded, and slowly backed up into a closet.

Not content with this response, I shoved a meter stick in the door, locking him in. I had my culprit, but justice had not been fully served. Our teacher, who had been absent through all of this, raced back into the classroom. "I heard a noise?"

Exasperated at his blasé attitude, I explained, "These three won't stop picking on Joseph. I took the law into my own hands because you won't do your job!"

At least, that's what I wish I had said, but I was a timid fifteen-year-old, so what actually came out was "... I locked Zack in the closet." Without looking at me, my teacher strolled toward the closet, with another meter stick in his hand, and shoved it into what little space was left between the first ruler and the door handle.

My first thought was, *You know what, Teach, you're all right,* but my second thought was, *This is crazy, we've got to get out of here!* The bell rang and I caught up with Joseph out in the hall. I reassured him that I was on his side and that I would try and pull some strings to get him into the Hub for the duration of each and every geography class for the rest of the year.

I went home and told my folks about what had happened and they sat down with my teacher to try and work out some strategies going forward. In the end, we didn't have to go anywhere; the three nitwits were sent to separate, isolated classrooms while Joseph and I carried out our studies in the geography classroom. I felt good about that, but then I thought, *maybe I enjoyed this class more when we weren't doing geography.*

All joking aside, I'd learned two things that year about teachers:

- They might not all be Saint Jeff, but even the bad ones are open to negotiation.

- It's important to stand up to authority when it's corrupt, but it's also important to understand how it became corrupt in the first place, so you can better reason with them. Sometimes they're scared because they don't know as much as the people they work for (the EA in the Hub); sometimes they're just sick and tired (the geography teacher).

Self-advocacy is an autistic person's best friend and an important concept for anyone with special challenges. In my experience, many students with ASD are inclined to work harder when you can collaborate with them and tailor a program to their skill set. Things like independent learning plans can be very helpful. The first step is just saying something. Find someone you can talk to (a teacher, student helper, or even the principal), let them know what your problem is, and talk about how you can deal with it. Be articulate and patient with them.

Self-advocacy is an autistic person's best friend and an important concept for anyone with special challenges.

Of course, you might not find a receptive ear with the first person you talk to—you may need to keep advocating to get what you need. And you need to balance your self-advocacy with reasonable expectations about what a teacher or a school can manage. Just remember that every time a system has changed for the better, it's because of someone saying, "I have a problem" loudly enough.

I bumped into Joseph just after school ended for the year. I was at my first ever Fan Expo, Canada's equivalent of the San Diego Comic-Con. He was there with a group I recognized from the Anime Club. He told me he had just gotten assessed for autism, which explained why he was there in the first place. I was happy for him. Autistic people need a tribe, and he had finally found his. As high school went on, I'd figure out what my tribe truly was, too.

Chapter 8

SOCIALLY AWKWARD MAN

Everyone has a hero growing up. But as an autistic kid in the early 2000s, there weren't many high-profile names attached to autism that I could look up to. Sure, we had the great Temple Grandin, but I just couldn't get into agriculture. Instead, I resolved to create my own hero. A superhero. One who represented the spectrum in all its glory. His name was …

SOCIALLY AWKWARD MAN!

Now, to fully appreciate Socially Awkward Man, you have to understand the very concept of "awkward."

Awkward. \ˈȯ-kwərd\. Adjective. A feeling of embarrassment, discomfort, or abnormality.

If music is the universal language, then awkward is the universal feeling. Awkward works in mysterious ways. Sometimes it's a handshake that was meant to be a high-five. Other times it's telling the guy who works at the movie theater to enjoy the movie, too. Awkward comes in so many forms: meeting your girlfriend's parents, getting socks as a birthday present, a friend request that turned out to be a computer virus, on and on and on.

Awkwardness might be the defining emotion of being on the spectrum. I myself am quite awkward, though my awkwardness was born out of the best of intentions. It's not that I had no social skills; it's just that my social skills put me out of step with the other kids of my generation. Holding the door for your classmates? Awkward. Smiling and using your manners? Awkward.

I believe people should be taught newer, more realistic social skills that go beyond "be nice and tell the truth." That said, people told me I would grow out of my awkwardness once I reached high school ... I'm still waiting.

I like to think Socially Awkward Man is a part of all of us. When you strive for perfection, you live in the shadow of potential failure. Humiliation. The fear that the second you mess up, no one will take you seriously anymore. Socially Awkward Man is the part of yourself that reminds you that we're all human. We all look a little stupid sometimes. At some point in your life, you will trip over backward, land in a puddle, and have people pointing and laughing at you. And that's okay. Socially Awkward Man says, "If you're going to stumble, do a pratfall!"

Don't fear awkwardness. Embrace it.

But, if you are looking for an airtight, foolproof plan for never feeling awkward again, try following this chart my friend made.

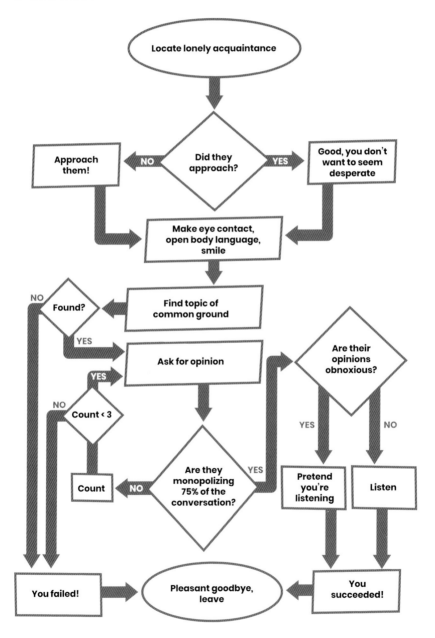

I think my awkwardness was a big part of why I gravitated so strongly to performing. An everyday, normal conversation was a kind of performance for me. Doing it onstage was somehow less exhausting, and much more rewarding.

Having spent most of my youth learning how to act, I found it challenging trying to assimilate myself into the neurotypical world. Most conversations with me sounded like bad line readings in a B-movie. But while I couldn't adequately impersonate natural behavior, I became much better at analyzing other people's behaviors. The micro stuff. Eye rolls. Wistful glances toward a phone or television set. I'd still lose people mid-sentence, but with my new, extensive knowledge of social skills, not only did I feel like I couldn't hold a conversation—I now had the proof to back it up.

However, by this point, I was doing comedy shows fairly regularly, and this skill was both useful and detrimental for a comic. Good because you can identify a member of your audience who might be a problem, but bad because you're so hung up on the jerk that you forget about everyone else who's laughing. It's a matter of ego. And it was really starting to affect my self-esteem.

I was struggling with my confidence offstage, too. In my life, I had always had a hard time finding a group where I really felt I belonged and was accepted. That's partly because in every group I found myself in, one person in that group would hate me.

Now, there are probably valid reasons to hate me. Maybe I stand way too close to people. Maybe they're annoyed that I talk in my "theater" voice all the time. Or is it the fact that I keep looping the conversation back to trains? It's happened throughout my life. It can't even be called bullying, really. It's subtler than that—just a quiet sigh when I walk in the room, or an eye roll every time I open my mouth to say something. Just a little something to let me know they can't stand me.

I shouldn't care about this. In a given group of, say, seven people, five out of the seven will like me. The only people who don't are this one person, and myself. So the math adds up. But with an ASD mind, you're always trying to solve problems. When you see a problem, you fixate on it and try to resolve it. But when there's no real reason for someone to hate you, there's nothing to solve. It's not even so much that you want to be liked; it's that you want to be understood by other people. And if your efforts at being understood are futile, then what's the point?

I've found many people with ASD have this in common: we obsess about the negative. You could have ten people complimenting the new streak you dyed in your hair, but if just one person says, "You look like a badger," that's the one you'll keep thinking about. Or, say someone holds a door for you and doesn't hear your thanks and then says, "You're welcome" in a loud, passive-aggressive voice. That kind of thing can hang like a cloud over me all day.

Aspies can really struggle with the casual callousness many people display. It's even more of a struggle when you know you're still upset about something most people would have already forgotten. Why do I let some guy's offhand comment ruin my day, or week?

I felt I had to combat this head-on; I couldn't let it stop me from doing the thing I loved. So I decided to do something where embarrassment was almost guaranteed. I dove head-first into the loopiest, most earnest-to-a-fault art form there was: musical theater. Having come a long way from my days of covering covers by the California Raisins, I was more than capable of carrying a tune. And holding a room, for that matter. My friend suggested I audition for a kitschy jukebox musical called *Back to the '80s*. I auditioned and got the lead.

For the most part, it was a wonderful experience. Many of my peers from drama class had been cast. There were some minor problems, although not unfamiliar ones. Much of the cast neglected to learn their lines. I had to grow a perm. And a few of the songs, most notably the Bonnie Tyler 1980s mega-hit power ballad, "Total Eclipse of the Heart," were teetering on the edge of my vocal range.

The show was a bundle of 80s cheese. There was a *Wonder Years*–style narration. (If you're not familiar with this 80s nostalgia-drenched sitcom, it was about a boy growing up in the 1960s and narrated by his philosophical older self. Kind of like *How I Met Your Mother.*) Everyone wore shoulder pads. My character dreamed about defeating the school bully in a lightsaber duel. It was all good fun. However, during the second show, something happened.

I am not unfamiliar with the second-show curse, wherein a cast gets a little too cocky after the success of their first performance and bungles the next one. This wasn't helped by me stupidly blowing out my voice box at the after party. I spent the next day *do-re-mi-fa-so-la-ti-do*-ing as hard as could, but I had to face facts ... "Total Eclipse of the Heart" was really going to suck that night.

The show started as expected. A mess. In the *Star Wars* dream sequence with the lightsaber duel, there's a point where the bully, dressed as Darth Vader, cuts my hand off. But this time, before the fight even started, I went to flick open the lightsaber and the saber part flew right off. In a moment of panic, I ripped off my false hand and beat him with it. If you've ever wanted to see a perplexed look on Darth Vader's helmet, you should've been there.

That wasn't the tough part, though. Alas, after the intermission, I would have to sing "Total Eclipse of the Heart," sounding a little more like Kim Carnes (another popular 1980s balladeer, known for her raspy vocal stylings) than Bonnie Tyler. First, a little context: in the aftermath of a wild party, my character, Corey, desperately tries to clean his house before his parents get home. While taking out the trash, he finds the girl of his dreams making out with his nemesis, Michael. Corey sings "Total Eclipse of the Heart."

While I was straining to hit the notes, I identified a small pocket in the audience, people my age, laughing hysterically. It terrified me. Unlike in stand-up, where I could react and talk back, I had to just commit to the material and take their reaction. Which was frustrating, because "Total Eclipse of the Heart" is a really long song. Not "Stairway to Heaven" long, but around six minutes.

I left the stage disheveled and found someone to vent my frustrations to. They explained to me that the hecklers were friends of the guy who played Michael and were laughing at the fact that he had just made out with someone onstage for six minutes while his girlfriend operated the spotlight. I said, "Oh ..."

It finally clicked that I can't live my life getting hung up on the thoughts of a select few. And that my keen assessments of human behavior might not always be that accurate. Some people have default expressions that make them look mean. Mine makes me look constipated. I get it.

> **It finally clicked that I can't live my life getting hung up on the thoughts of a select few.**

I've gotten better over the years at dealing with my fear that people will hate me, and one thing that helps is the knowledge that a certain percentage of the people you encounter are always going to hate you, and for no particular reason. It's going to be a constant through your life. Once you come to grips with this knowledge, it's liberating. You're not afraid of trying to appease people and make them like you, because you know you can't. It might sound nihilistic, but in this instance, resignation will save you.

My acting career didn't continue for much longer. A friend advised that I get an agent. I got taken out of high school to go play an extra on *Degrassi*, which is like getting out of jury duty to go play a member of a jury. Luckily, I had the experience to make the role believable. I was glad to act again, if only to realize how little I knew about how other people think and what it was like to live without fear.

Chapter 9

CINEMA du AUTISM

In the opening scene of *Blade Runner*, Ridley Scott's sci-fi/film noir hybrid, a genetically engineered android, called a replicant, is taken into a room and asked a series of questions designed to tell robots from humans. The questions are meant to stimulate an emotional response, and if the replicant doesn't respond in the correct way, they'll be executed.

The first time I watched this scene, I had just turned fifteen, and it triggered something in me. I'm not a robot (as far as I know) and I'm not on the run from the government (yet). But it took me back to a time when I was also being asked questions intended to provoke an emotional response and scared of getting the answers wrong because I just wasn't wired that way (literally, in the case of the Blade Runner). The image haunted me.

I identified with the replicants, the robots who were being interrogated and hunted down. To me, the movie was about people being persecuted because they didn't fit a conventional neurological model. *Blade Runner* taught me true empathy. It also taught me how to read a film.

I had loved all sorts of movies since I was very young, and there were plenty of movies up until that point where I enjoyed the characters and story. But *Blade Runner* was the first that really made me question its purpose. Why did the director make these choices? Why was this image juxtaposed with that one? Why was this scene lit in this way to evoke this mood?

Movies have also done a lot to shape the public's perception of autism—the most famous being *Rain Man*, the 1988 movie about an autistic savant played by Dustin Hoffman. We're at a point now where we have autistic lead characters in films that aren't even about autism. *The Accountant*, for example.

I don't think these representations are inaccurate, necessarily—in all fairness, they feel like the writers talked to experts and researched their subject. But the characters often seem like a checklist of symptoms rather than real people, a collection of quirks that have been mistaken for a personality. The problem with presenting autism on-screen is that it becomes the crux of the character. Having autism is a characteristic, not a character.

The Jim Henson Company, which has been rightly lauded for doing its research, worked with the Autism Self Advocacy Network to create Julia, the autistic character on *Sesame Street*.

Part of the reason her portrayal was so revolutionary was that the writers didn't go to researchers—they went directly to people with autism. Having people with ASD in the writers' room is a huge deal, and it helps create something honest and lived-in.

I'm glad to know that we have so many films coming out right now starring autistic heroes. And these aren't sob stories about a person at war with themselves—they're big-budget action movies! One of these heroes is a Power Ranger, for crying out loud.

We're finally shifting away from stories where the main villain in an autistic person's story is their own autism. Now the bad guy is an institution that refuses to accommodate them, in shows like *The Good Doctor* for example.

As for the individuals themselves, they've learned to turn a perceived handicap into a strength. One might even call it a superpower.

Fueled by my appreciation of *Blade Runner*, my obsession with movies only continued to grow. This passion ended up being convenient for my folks, because they were looking for a camp to ship me off to for the summer. They shrugged: "Well, I guess it's going to be film camp." It turned out to be not only a way for me to pursue my love of movies, but the answer to my quest for a tribe.

One week into July, my folks made the muggy trek into Canada's Niagara region to drop me off at camp. Within moments of my arrival, the locals, campers and counselors alike, embraced me with open arms. My folks could sleep knowing I was in good hands, and once I got there, I didn't look back.

This camp was unlike anything I'd ever experienced. Each night, they held pop-culture-themed dinners where the entire staff would dress up and walk around in character. For instance, the first night of the summer was a *Seinfeld*-themed buffet, where the whole camp lined up outside of the dining hall and never got to go inside.

I loved it, and I can still remember those nights like they were yesterday, which is easy because this all happened less than a decade ago.

That was how we spent our nights, whereas our days were made up of extensive film studies ("This is how you turn on a camera") and intellectual discussions in the quad ("I like how Stanley Kubrick turns on a camera").

What was most intriguing to me about this camp was how open people were to discussing their mental health. It wasn't specifically a camp for kids with diagnoses, but there happened to be a lot of us there with neurological or mental health differences. And it was a completely stigma-free zone. As a matter of fact, when it came time to grab your meds from the nurse's cabin, there was a lineup nearly half a mile long, full of kids discussing, without judgment, their respective disorders. This was a completely new thing for me.

So we bonded over our interests and similarities in more ways than one. I had already experienced being part of a group with the fellow ASD kids at my school, but this felt different— our shared passion for film was creatively inspiring and exciting in a new way for me. And these kids were different from any friends I'd ever had. They were mostly a bit older than me, artsy, and cool. Camp became a home away from home, and when the summer came to an end, we couldn't bear to part with each other. I held on to the naive belief that we'd all stay in contact, despite the fact that I lived in Ontario and my friends lived in Europe. "We'll keep it to monthly meetups," I'd say to them.

I handed around a piece of paper that all my friends could fill in with their contact info. But when I got it back, there weren't any phone numbers on it. Just names. "Add me on Facebook," they said. I didn't know what Facebook was.

I wasn't so behind the times that I could only communicate via messenger pigeon, but my family had only gotten Internet the previous year. Heck, I didn't even get a cell phone until much later, and that was at my folks' request. Basically, if you weren't on a landline, you'd never hear from me again.

And yet, I wanted to keep chasing the unobtainable goal of hanging out with my new friends before the next summer vacation. I got myself a Facebook account and began my long trek into darkness.

Introducing Team Spectrum

As I noted in the previous chapter, the autism community is really strapped for heroic representation, at least on the comic book superhero front. I wish to rectify this. Introducing ...

Master and commander
of the conversation. His
power is also his weakness!

She wouldn't mind the cape if
there wasn't a tag in the back.

She's never quite sure if
what she heard was a joke or
not, so she'll laugh anyway!

He's a real slam dunk
when it comes to being
waaaaaay too close.

He's not flailing for help;
it's just something he does.

As in, he is very literal,
and also a man.

Before I go any further, I want to make it clear that I'm not going on some diatribe about how technology is the devil and it's ruined my generation. I honestly feel that the Internet has been especially helpful for people with autism. Websites like

Wrong Planet have provided a space where folks on the spectrum can congregate without the typical anxieties that come with real-life social interactions.

"He keeps checking his phone! Does he hate me?!" You know the kind.

These days any Aspie with an Internet connection can make a four-thousand-word post about science, politics, or a minor *Star Wars* character and have an audience willing to engage with them, which very much beats trying to find a person in real life who will listen to you monologue about such subjects for half an hour. When I first got on social media, I had a field day. Suddenly this gate opened up to a world where I could meet all these people with similar hobbies and interests, and talk ad nauseam about Pokémon, dinosaurs, and the color green ... or so I thought.

As it turned out, talking to people online isn't all that different from talking to people in person. People on Facebook don't have time to discuss why a Liopleurodon is better than a T. rex. They've got maybe four minutes to update their relationship status, "like" a video of a cockatoo screaming into an eggshell, and then move on with their lives.

After a while, I gave up on further communications with my new camp friends. It wasn't their fault, but an electronic interface was no substitute for chatting with them in person. And besides, this was at a point where phones weren't quite mini-computers yet. Texting took forever, and people had lives to attend to.

At this point in my journey, a sane person would have accepted reality and waited until the next summer to hang with their camp peeps. I, instead, went another route: I would find replicas of my camp friends. I would befriend cool, older artsy people at school, and maybe I could recreate the magic I found at camp.

At the annual Halloween dance, I found a group that fit the bill. I had come dressed as Dog the Builder, the failed offspring of Dog the Bounty Hunter and Bob the Builder. I found them by the door, dressed as the Droogs from *A Clockwork Orange*, doing an ironic send-up of the Cha-Cha Slide. That gave me an opening to talk to them about Stanley Kubrick and film, and we hit it off.

The next day, I found myself spending lunch with this ragtag group, where I pitched to them my idea for a gritty sequel to my grade three *SpongeBob* play: an apocalyptic drama set during the BP oil spill. (The twist: Dennis isn't dead!) It felt just like film camp. And before I knew it, this had become my lunchtime ritual.

As for my Aspie crew, our mutual interests began to diverge; nobody there was into film the way my new pals and I were. I stopped going to Anime Club. I didn't even drop by the Hub. While everyone there was talking about the latest trend in gaming, I was at the library, immersing myself in whatever world cinema I could get my hands on.

We barely hung out for a year, which is a shame, because if there is anything you can count on an Aspie for, it's punctuality. Whereas my new artsy surrogates were a little more … flippant. They were by no means bad people, but in hindsight, they were a little less keen on hanging out with me than I was on hanging out with them.

For instance, each night after school, I'd inbox my artsy film group with a simple proposition: "Hey gang! Wanna hang this weekend?" It wouldn't take long for my nemesis to appear: the "seen at" sign. It was the first of several crushing reminders that even though the group had received my message, they still had better things to do.

I'd retaliate by sending another message, this one a little more desperate. Something along the lines of: "It's cool if you don't. Maybe the weekend after?"

The "seen at" sign would come on again. Then its evil sidekick, the "typing" symbol, would take its place to give me the false hope that maybe, just maybe, someone would answer me. But they didn't. The "seen at" sign would return.

Time passes. The "seen at" sign tells me it's been thirty minutes since the message was seen. Then it tells me it's been two hours. Realizing this hangout is not in the stars, I panic and begin cranking out paragraph after paragraph about how my life's been, what new show I'm watching, how overrated I think insert-director's-name-here is. Nothing.

This is the last I'd ever hear from them …

… until four hours later. One response: "Sorry, dude. I'm

swamped this week."

I say, "No prob!"

End of conversation.

I regret to admit that this had become my new nightly routine. During that time, several members of my old Aspie crew reached out to me, and like an idiot, I dismissed them. Because I was waiting for what my dad calls "the better offer," which is when you give a "maybe" to someone, not because you have plans, but because you're waiting for something more exciting to pop up. In public school, I had been on the receiving end of this treatment, and now I was doing it to my own friends.

I learned as well that the neurotypical high school kids were a lot more blasé about plans than I was, and having a piece of technology as efficient as a cell phone in their pockets just made it worse. As someone with autism, I need closure. I need a concrete understanding that if we plan to meet somewhere at a certain time, it's going to happen, and that if you need to cancel, you'll notify me as early as possible. But a lot of people don't think that way, because they have this device that lets them contact someone immediately, anytime.

Cell phones can make people feel that it's fine to cancel plans at the last minute. They think, "I can call you the second we're supposed to meet and say, 'Whoops, I slept through my alarm.'" I had just gotten my phone and I didn't know these rules. I also didn't have a driver's license, so over and over I would find myself stranded in town waiting for someone who was never going to arrive. Things like that strained my relationship with my new high school crew, and eventually prevented me from getting too close to them.

It took me a while to learn this, but I finally realized that the people who matter are the ones who make time for you. Friendship is deeper than having mutual interests. Friendship is setting aside time in your day to help someone forget about life for a while.

Friendship is deeper than having mutual interests.

In May, I returned to the Hub, hat in hand. My Aspie gang embraced me with open arms. It was like I had never left. I could hear the faint strains of Elvis Costello from down the hall where the artsy crew was hanging out. I wished them the best, then shut the door behind me.

That summer, I went back to film camp, but I didn't take down any names at the end. I went in knowing that the limited time I had with these people was precious and I should spend it enjoying myself instead of worrying about the chilling absence that would come afterward.

Oh my god, I just got the ending to *Blade Runner*!

Chapter 10

SAY (LITERALLY) ANYTHING

Subtext has never been my strong suit. It's often difficult for me to tell if someone is joking or not. Double meanings have plagued me since my friend's eighth birthday party. We were having a water-balloon fight. I refused to throw my balloon because it was green, my favorite color. One of the parents told me to "just run with it." So I did … all the way through the suburbs. It took them two hours to find me.

Literal language means exactly what it says. Figurative language, on the other hand, paints word pictures and allows us to "see" a point. It uses similes, metaphors, and hyperbole to describe something, often by comparing it to something different. Figurative language is great for poetry, but not so easy for people on the spectrum.

Sarcasm is also difficult for many autistic people; it's often cued by someone's tone of voice, which is hard for us to recognize. I have a hard time understanding sarcasm unless someone is really obvious about it. "Were they serious?" is a recurring thought of mine.

When you talk to someone with ASD, try to use literal terms and direct language. And remember that they may need a little help to understand the importance of tone and nonverbal communication in conversation.

As a part of our literal-mindedness, many of us on the spectrum are sticklers for the truth. If someone asks for our opinion, we're inclined to give it to them, unabridged, because we respect their intelligence. That said, there is a world of difference between honesty and unsolicited comments. I, like many a person with autism, have found this out the hard way. For Aspies, it's good to remind ourselves to think before we speak. While it's fine to be upfront with what you want from people, sometimes being too upfront can put people off.

It's all part of communication, which is something I, and many of my Aspie buds, have struggled with. For instance, we can be too specific in some areas, while not being specific enough in others. It's gotten me into trouble. Most significantly, in my romantic life.

There are a lot of media stereotypes about how autistic people handle romantic relationships. I think people imagine that an Aspie can't really fall in love the same way as other people, that we're too emotionless or neurotic. In fact, as I've said before, people with autism do have the capacity to feel—

in fact, we often feel so much at once that we shut down as a coping mechanism. Also, we don't always assign the right meaning to our feelings.

My first girlfriend from back in grade three (who, as we've already established, wasn't really my girlfriend) taught me an awful lot about what I was looking for in a relationship, which was, simply enough, someone to hang out with. This ideal was shaped by what I observed in my parents' relationship, which had never been one of holding hands and bringing each other flowers. Instead, they liked to crack wise while sharing a beer on the porch. I figured being in a relationship was sort of like being in a buddy cop movie. You just make quips and tolerate each another.

> **I figured being in a relationship was sort of like being in a buddy cop movie. You just make quips and tolerate each another.**

I never had trouble finding a girlfriend. I was very extroverted: I was loud and over-the-top, and people liked to watch me perform. But eventually they would get sick of me. The ones who fell for the performer would soon discover I wasn't like that all the time—when I'm not "on," I'm rather boring. Once they caught on to that, they'd usually dump me. Only the communication in my relationships was so lacking that I didn't always know I'd been dumped.

Here's one example. This goes back to the summer of 2009. School was out, and I'd started dating a girl I met at a day camp. Things seemed to be going well. But then, something must have changed. What it was, I did not know, because she didn't actually break up with me. She just stopped returning my calls, with no explanation.

Finally, after two months, I decided to break the silence and give her a call. Preferably, I would've liked to have coordinated a face-to-face meeting where we could agree on an amicable separation. The idea of breaking up over the phone always seemed rude to me, but it was the only way to get closure. I mustered the courage to call.

"Hello?" she answered.

"Hey! So, are we broken up?" I said.

And she said, "Oh! I forgot to tell you."

And that was the end of it.

The following summer, the same thing happened again, with another girl. She suddenly stopped returning my calls. Then I heard through a friend that she wanted to break up with me, but her mother had told her it would break my heart…

…what?

By the time I was in high school, I hadn't had a relationship for quite some time, but I was surrounded by people I liked. On top of that, I'd seen how friend groups could implode once people started dating within it. It made the most sense to avoid dating for a while.

And then, in grade eleven, I began dating a girl outside of my friend ecosystem. I liked her and enjoyed her company, but I continued to struggle with something called "nice one-upmanship." It's when someone gives you a compliment, and you think, *That's such a good compliment. I need to give you a better one!* And then you do. But then they give you a better compliment. So you give them a better compliment. On and on and on ...

Let me set the stage. We'd gone to her cottage for the weekend. It was the Saturday night, and we were watching the sun set, cracking wise while sharing a ginger ale on the porch. My folks would've been proud. Until this exchange happened:

Her: "You know what? I love hanging out with you."

Me: "Yeah, I could do this FOREVER."

She didn't talk to me for the remainder of the trip.

After a week's time, I gave her a call. "I feel like I scared you off. That wasn't my intention, but if you don't want to go out anymore, I understand."

But she remained dismissive: "I'm sorry, but we're just not compatible. What's a good analogy ...? Have you ever seen a web comic called *Homestuck*?"

"No," I replied.

She continued, "Okay, so at the start of act one—"

Apparently, we were like a something-troll and a

something-sprite. We could never be together for we weren't cut from the same cloth. Instead of just saying that, she recapped the entire plot of *Homestuck*, which, according to Wikipedia, is longer than the Bible. By the time she had finished, I had mostly forgotten that I just got dumped.

And that's what happens when Aspies date.

My communication woes were not exclusive to romance. Nor was I always on the receiving end. Now, I'd like to talk about a certain kind of communication breakdown. One that comes from being too specific in your demands, to the point that people can't tell if you're serious or joking. I'll give you an example, and like the previous story, this one requires some background.

It was the mid 2000s. Beyblades had just been banned at my school for being literally spinning tops with knives on them, and now Yu-Gi-Oh! was the hip new game you could gamble your lunch money on. To clarify, Yu-Gi-Oh! was like Pokémon for nerds. When *Yu-Gi-Oh! The Movie* finally came to town, there were sold-out shows every night of the week. To be fair, my town only had a two-screen cinema and the other movie was *The Time Traveler's Wife*, so ...

My friends and I didn't want to put up with all the crying babies and couples whispering, "Who's he again?" so we resolved to go splitsies on a DVD copy of *Yu-Gi-Oh! The Movie* the second it hit the shelves. My friend Lewis had the honor of picking up the flick from what was then known as "Not Quite Dead Yet" Blockbuster Video.

Lewis was an interesting fellow. He was great at advocating for himself. Perhaps a little too much so. If he needed something, no matter how specific, he'd ask for it and would ensure he got it. That's the kind of due diligence that made General Patton a great leader on the battlefield but was probably also what made him awkward to be around in elementary school.

Let me set the scene. The gang and I were chilling in Lewis's living room. The movie was cued up, and the popcorn had just entered the microwave. We were all stoked! Lewis returned with a bowl of popcorn in one hand and the remote in the other. My other friend Jackson called out, "Play the movie!"

Lewis responded, "First, some ground rules ..."

Lewis had come prepared with a list of oddly specific requests. According to him, we were to only take one piece of popcorn at a time. If we took so much as two pieces, he would stop the movie and restart it from the beginning.

We thought he was joking. What fools we were. Not one minute in, Jackson's hand plunged into the bowl of popcorn and returned with a fistful of kernels. As promised, Lewis stopped the movie, then restarted it from the beginning.

We hadn't expected Lewis to actually follow through on his joke. But such is the way of any good joke—you don't expect the punchline. Everyone laughed ... except Lewis.

Take 2. We got to the exact same point in the movie as

last time when once again, Jackson took another handful of popcorn. Once again, Lewis stopped the movie and went back to the beginning.

That's when we lost our minds. "Why are you rationing popcorn?" we screamed. "There's only three of us!"

Yet the only people we really had to blame were ourselves. Lewis had been totally upfront about his stance on popcorn, and might have been open for discussion, but we hadn't taken him seriously. We should have believed him when he told us what he needed.

Fast-forward to 2012. Lewis and I, after years of silence, begin speaking again. One day I build up the courage to ask him, "Do you still have the Yu-Gi-Oh! movie?"

He nods sheepishly. "It's pretty bad," he says. "I don't think you could sit through it."

I retort, "I will if I can eat more than one popcorn at a time."

He doesn't laugh. We haven't spoken since.

To this day, I have never seen anything past the opening credits of *Yu-Gi-Oh! The Movie*.

Communication's a two-way street. Not all of the blame can fall squarely on the giver or the recipient (regardless of each's neurological wiring). What we have to do is be understanding of one another, not judge others exclusively by our own experience, and, to quote my mom, shut up and listen.

Chapter 11

THE QUEST FOR IMMORTALITY

By grade twelve I saw fit to end my high school career with a bang. I'd begun masterminding a showcase for myself that, until this point, had been years in the making.

Since the beginning of high school, I had been performing stand-up at a series of autism-based functions. (My jokes were exclusively about autism. Everything you've read up to this point? That's what I talked about.) And yet, while I was technically a professional comedian, my inability to score gigs in the clubs left me feeling inadequate. While another, more thoughtful teenage comic might have deduced that they couldn't get into a club because they were underage, I jumped to the self-loathing conclusion that it was because I'd become a hack who relied exclusively on his autism for material.

My head was clouded with intrusive thoughts like *Am I a comic, or am I an autism advocate who tells some jokes? And if I am an advocate, could I be a good comic, too? Am I even that good of an advocate? Why are people laughing at me, anyway? Is it pity? Or secondhand embarrassment?*

A friend of a friend referred me to a master class comedian who could lend me some insight. I booked a lunch with him and used the opportunity to lay out my concerns, which mostly revolved around how I was worried that my act built around having autism had become a gimmick. He gave me a very sage piece of advice:

"Hang on to that gimmick with your life!"

My response was mixed. While he definitely had a point, I still needed to prove things to myself. I needed to know that I could get out there on my own and succeed on my own merits.

It was in that precise moment that I decided to undertake the most ambitious project of my life: a cross-Canada tour.

Correction … A DOCUMENTARY ABOUT MY FIRST EVER CROSS-CANADA TOUR!

I was disgustingly vain. I mean, what idiot thinks they're interesting enough to carry a whole documentary when they're eighteen? I guess the same idiot who thinks it's appropriate to write a memoir at age twenty-two.

With help from my folks and several autism-based charities, I was able to book a gig in every province across the country. My dad had the connections to book the gigs and my mom handled the logistics of where to stay and how to get there, so I was free to focus on preparing for the shows. We would be flying from Toronto to St. John's, Newfoundland, to start the tour, then to Halifax for the next show. After that, we would pick up an RV and drive it all the way to Vancouver. All in all, it would be a month-long tour.

In the meantime, I had to get good with a camera. Fall was fast approaching, and I needed the doc to look good, or, at the very least, competent. Film camp had taught me a thing or two about lighting and composition, but next to nothing about documentary filmmaking.

Luckily, the local Rogers Community Television Centre was willing to take me under their wing as part of their co-op program for high school students. I approached the opportunity with a little too much arrogance. Having spent many a sick day at home watching *Maury*, I figured I knew everything I needed to know about producing daytime television.

The producers were impressed at my Forrest Gump–like ability to set up a camera in seconds flat, and annoyed at my complete inability to take it apart. I was kind of like the Glass Half Full personified. Not because I'm an optimist, but because I'm a disappointing alternative to a full glass. My ego had been knocked down a peg. There was still much to learn.

My overlords were benevolent. Strict, but fair. They taught me everything from how to direct a live show in studio, to reporting out in the field, to catching a scoop before your competition. I looked like a maniac as I raced around town, camera in hand, searching for something interesting to happen. I was like that guy from *Nightcrawler*, but with his mom driving him everywhere.

By the end of the semester, I had produced two six-episode TV shows. I was quite proud of the first show. It was a documentary series about senior citizens who had contributed greatly to our community. One of them was a former Buckingham Palace guard during the Second World War, and another one was the coach of the local special-needs hockey team, who gave me a testimonial that to this day still puts a lump in my throat.

The second show was a variety show about creative, artsy types in the community. While it was not without its moments, each and every episode ended with an ill-advised segment known as "Explain It to Me Like I'm Six," where I'd interview a six-year-old girl, also named Michael, about some sort of field trip she went on, whilst playing footage from the adventure (trip to a horse ranch, a reptile exhibit, etc.). On paper, it sounded adorable and funny; in practice ... well, W.C. Fields said, "Never work with children or animals." I like to live dangerously, so I worked with both.

It was all my fault. When my mom pitched the idea to me, I hadn't considered the fact that maybe the kid would have way more fun going out in the field and riding horses than she would talking about it in a small, dank studio. The results were hilarious for all the wrong reasons.

For the first and only day of filming, other Michael arrived beaming, the most charismatic kid you've ever met. Eager to tell us all about her many quests. The second my producer flipped on the "on air" light, something inside her died.

The interview began: "And we're back in the studio with me and my sidekick, Other Michael. How are you doin', Other Michael?"

Silence from Other Michael.

"Nope ..."

More silence.

"Okay, let's get things started." My producer cut to the footage, which now had some sort of Kenny G–style elevator music overtop. After a five-second pause, he screamed into my headset, "Speak!"

And I did. "Looks like you were at a horse ranch. Did you get to ride one?" She nodded her head. "I guess you did. Was it fun?" She shrugged. "A little scary?" She shrugged again. "You're smiling in the video."

I answered my own questions for thirty minutes. Sure, it was spread across six five-minute segments, but in TV time, that's an eternity. I suddenly knew how the Lego Lady felt.

It was a failure. But one that lit a fire in my belly. I would not let "Explain It to Me Like I'm Six" be my legacy. And now I had some documentary experience under my belt, which would be crucial in achieving my next professional goal ... the tour and documentary.

In the meantime, I had one more obstacle: HIGH SCHOOL GRADUATION. My last semester had a few twists and turns in it. I was nominated for valedictorian, which was strange, because I had literally locked a guy in a closet four years prior. But I was excited to learn that valedictorians were voted in by students rather than teachers. Even more exciting, it turned out my best friend from drama class—one of the same friends from the great *Yu-Gi-Oh!* caper—had single-handedly gotten me the nomination, which put me in debt to him forever. We're roommates now. That's not a joke.

It's one thing to do a favor for a friend, but it's another thing to help your friend realize their dream (er, one of them). The dream in question? Well, it wasn't becoming valedictorian. My dream was far more ambitious. See, at this high school, the valedictorian would give their commencement speech in front of a giant grad photo of themselves, straight-up *Citizen Kane*–style. So I knew that if I won, I'd get to speak in front of this …

I didn't get valedictorian, though. Sadly, the universe is ever-expanding and didn't care about my stupid joke. Instead, I received a plaque for something about ladder safety. God forbid my roommate's ever in a stepladder accident, because I am now legally responsible for his life.

There is really nothing more polarizing than high school memories, eh? Some get caught up reliving their glory days, and others are stuck on missed opportunities—should they have asked that person out? Should they have stood up to that bully? I opt for a more bipartisan view. Was high school tedious? A bit. Were there jerks? Of course, but there were plenty of nice people, teachers and students alike. I suppose what I'm trying to say is, while I might have checked out the second I decided to pursue comedy—which, mind you, was before grade nine even began—I have no regrets. They were a silly four years, and I'll remember them fondly, if at all.

But enough pontificating. After commencement, I found myself with much bigger fish to fry.

September rolled around. We had everything we needed for the tour. A Winnebago, a dashcam, two camcorders, and enough frozen pizza to get ourselves through the month. My mom, dad, and best friend from school—also autistic—were along for the trip, and my older brother, who had moved out west, would be joining us once we got to Alberta. My dad was the sole driver of the Winnebago. He said the monotony kept him calm, which was good, because he would need to save up that calm for when he eventually had to plow through the Rockies overnight in blizzard weather. I slept through that terrifying event and woke up in Vancouver the next morning, ignorant to the fact that we almost died fifteen times the evening prior.

Unfortunately for me, I wasn't asleep for all the hard parts. As a matter of fact, one show was a particularly grueling experience. It was in the Maritimes, which was terrifying, because I went out there knowing the audience was already funnier than me. The opening act had killed with some regional humor, which the audience loved. But I wasn't from 'round there, and when I went up and did the first joke, there was complete silence.

I did the second joke. Again, nothing. I stood on the stage, looking out into pitch darkness.

I had to do a thirty-minute set.

It's one thing to have people boo you—a producer will forgive you if you cut your losses and get offstage quick. At least they can salvage the show. But what do you do when people are totally silent?

But I kept going, telling my jokes, one after the other, getting absolutely nothing back every time. After what seemed like an eternity, I finished my last joke.

"All right, guys, thank you for coming out!" I said wearily.

And then, completely out of nowhere, I received the longest standing ovation of my career.

At the time I figured it was because they were so grateful I was done. "Thank God! We get to go home now." But after the show, people started coming up to me, wanting to take photos.

"Hey, get a picture of me and the guy with autism!"

"We loved your show! It was really inspirational!"

They had been really moved by my act, even if they hadn't laughed. It wasn't exactly the reaction I had been hoping for, but since then, I've learned that if someone gives you a compliment, you shut up and take it. At the time, though, I took it and then pouted in the RV for the next twenty-four hours.

See, I was still hung up on the word "inspirational." It's ironic that a word meaning "to give others the urge to create" has such a negative connotation in the world of performing. When a person hears the word "inspirational," they don't think of George Carlin. They think of Tony Robbins. At eighteen, I didn't want to be inspirational; I just wanted to be funny. That said, "motivational" and "inspirational" are two totally different things. Okay, according to the Google dictionary, they're not, but I'm getting off track.

As the tour went farther west, people laughed at my stuff, but the "I" word began popping up more and more. At that point, I stopped minding so much, though. In fact, I figured I should be more grateful. Many of the shows I was doing were for autism organizations, so my audiences were mostly autistic people and families with autistic children. I learned that it's one thing to have people come up to you and say, "You're really funny." But it's another thing to have them say, "You gave me hope for my kid."

> **I learned that it's one thing to have people come up to you and say, "You're really funny." But it's another thing to have them say, "You gave me hope for my kid."**

I performed my last set in Vancouver to my smallest crowd. It was made up of some extended family and my older brother's new B.C. friends. I couldn't have felt more at home. After the show, I reviewed some of the footage from the tour. To put it frankly, there was nothing. No story. No real conflict. Just a lot of driving (most of it through Saskatchewan).

I resolved that the tour would be not the focal point of the doc, but merely its starting point. The first step toward a greater, decade-spanning epic. Since the tour, I've been filming everything I do. Everything. Like these words you are currently reading. I'm filming them as I type them. How freakin' meta is that!

… I'll never finish this movie …

But I will finish this book!

I must have, or else you wouldn't be reading it. But please, don't stop.

PART 3

STIM CITY

My whole life I fretted over the prospect of independence. My older brother left for Vancouver the moment he graduated high school, and my younger brother resigned himself to the fact that he could never live on his own.

I was caught in the middle. Not totally complacent living with my folks, but ultimately terrified of not knowing how to function separate from them. Despite their apprehension, as well as my own, I decided to conquer my fear by facing it head-on: move out to Toronto on my own to try to make it in comedy.

Something every young adult on the spectrum has to work out for themselves is how independent they can be going into the future. Those are questions an ASD person's family will turn over in their minds from the moment of diagnosis. Of course, there are many people on the spectrum who are able to live independently, have careers, and support themselves just like a neurotypical person. But though independence is often seen as a goal, it's just not possible for some on the spectrum, like my brother. Still others will end up on a middle ground, with a balance of independent activities and support from family or others. It's all about finding what works for you— doing what you're capable of, but not hesitating to ask for the help you need.

I started making baby steps toward becoming a self-sustaining, independent young man on the spectrum: moving out, getting my first job, and building my comedy career.

Chapter 12

GOOD COP, TRANSIT COP

Two months after my cross-Canada tour, I began taking biweekly improv classes in Toronto. The big smoke. Home to *Degrassi*, Honest Ed's, and "Please Dismount" signs that cyclists never pay attention to.

There was some culture shock, yes, but I had to endure. I was out of school, a semi-adult, and my eventual goal was to live full time in the big city. If I screwed up now, I assumed my folks would never have enough faith in me to let me live on my own. I'm extremely lucky in that they have always had my back and supported me in everything I've done, from my earliest peer interactions at school, to my theatrical creations, to my tour. They helped make all those things happen for me. But that meant that I had never really done anything completely on my own. So I needed to prove myself capable of functioning on my own—to my folks, and to myself.

I was still living with my parents in Orangeville at the time, but commuting to the city by transit every day for improv classes at the legendary Second City theater. For a little over a month, I had been doing okay. I made it thirty-three days without having a major problem.

On the thirty-fourth day, I was summoned to court.

Here's how it happened. I liked the efficiency of not having to pay a fare every time I used transit, so every month, I'd save up to buy a TTC Metropass, which enabled me to hop on any streetcar or subway without a thought.

But I wanted to make sure I was using the pass correctly and not missing any nuances. With an ASD mind, you get good at reading the fine print. In the past I'd been screwed over by taking things at face value. As a result, I became very anal-retentive and required clarification on everything. Like I said, specificity is an Aspie's best friend. This time, though, it backfired on me.

I investigated the TTC website and it said that you could purchase a monthly pass as early as the twenty-fifth day of the previous month and up to four days into the following month. What this meant, of course, was that you could buy a pass for the NEW month up to four days into that month. But at no point did the wording convey the obvious information that your monthly pass expired at the end of said month. The way my brain perceived this was that I had a four-day grace period with the previous month's pass. This led to my ill-fated decision to go into the city to get my new pass on the fourth.

On that day, I got on the bus with my last month's pass and showed it to the driver. At this point he could have stopped me and cleared up my misconception; I would have gladly paid the fare and we would have been square. But he let me get on, anyway. I kept riding until we got to the station in Toronto. I got off, and two transit cops were waiting there to check passes. And when they got to me and saw my four-day-expired pass, they stopped me and took me aside.

Now, I'm sympathetic to transit cops. It's got to be the most boring, soul-sucking job in the world. They spend most of their days yelling at high school students trying to game the transit system and the rest of the time in a dank, pee-smelling basement doing paperwork. So I could tell they were relishing the opportunity to put the screws to an actual adult (just barely, but still). They were about to give me the shakedown. (And by shakedown, I mean a $200 fine.)

"On the first day of the month, we'd maybe let it slide," the first transit cop said, doing his best *Goodfellas* impression.

"Yeah," his partner agreed.

"On the second day—eh, kind of pushing it. Maybe." Cop 1 went on, "But on day four? Uh-uh. No way."

I was on the verge of a nervous breakdown.

"Sorry," I said, shaking. "I—I guess there was a misunderstanding."

"You betcha!" they said.

And then I revealed, "I have autism spectrum disorder."

And like that, they deflated. "Oh, God" expressions stretched across their faces. Clearly wanting to get me out of there as quickly as possible and avoid a PR nightmare, they handed me a piece of paper with a phone number for the court, telling me I could call and negotiate the terms of the ticket. The implication being: "Please don't tell anyone about this."

Huh, I thought, walking out of there. *That went quickly from the worst day of my life to not so bad.* I got out of the incident mostly okay, but I walked away with a lesson in how systems can fail people who aren't neurotypical. In this case, I had gone looking for some simple information, and not only did I not get answers, I didn't receive help until it was much too late.

As I was still living at home in Orangeville, I had the option of negotiating the fine in phone court. But at that point I was ready to pay up and avoid humiliating myself any further. Mostly, I didn't want to tell my folks about it. I didn't want them to know I had failed at being an adult.

Now, my own misconceptions about the situation were not helping me here. Over the past month, my parents had been very vigilant about my activities in the city. They just wanted to be involved and make sure I was doing okay, but in my mind, they were testing me—if I showed my incompetence at adulting, they'd think I wasn't ready to live on my own. It turned out they didn't actually think that way at all, and if I had actually talked to them and consulted them for advice, it might have saved me some angst. I thought that being a technical adult meant I had to go from the frying pan straight into the fire and I wasn't allowed to ask for help ever again.

Anyway, the truth all came out at dinner that night. My mom asked, going straight for the jugular, "Did you get your new pass?" And I, being more transparent than cellophane, proceeded to tell her everything. It didn't matter to me if she gave me her infamous hairy eyeball; I just wanted to put the whole thing behind me.

> **I thought that being a technical adult meant I had to go from the frying pan straight into the fire and I wasn't allowed to ask for help ever again.**

But she listened and wasn't judgmental. Instead, she insisted she call the phone court, argue my case, and give them hell for the unhelpful way the system had treated me. My mom: the spitting image of Erin Brockovich.

Initially, I was embarrassed by the thought of having my folks, yet again, fight my battles for me. But then again, I was also embarrassed by my own inability to emotionally cope with what was basically a parking ticket. I gave my mom the number and paced anxiously in the living room.

She explained to the prosecutor what had happened.

"When did he get the ticket?" he asked.

"On the fourth," she said.

"Well, there you have it," he said. "You've got to pay the fine."

"Well …," my mom said, and launched into my defense. But he wouldn't budge.

"Fine, screw it, I'll pay the fine," she sighed at last.

But then another voice came on the line. A woman's voice. Unbeknownst to my mom, she had been listening the whole time. "Before you settle this, do you have anything to declare?"

My mom, not realizing she was talking to the judge, said, "Yeah, I do," and gave them a piece of her mind. She complained about the unclear wording and the way I'd been treated by the transit cops.

The judge agreed. "Well, gee, that sounds like one big misunderstanding. I think he's learned his lesson, and if it doesn't happen again, no harm done!"

"But it was the fourth!" the prosecutor wailed fruitlessly.

But the judge had already reached her verdict. "Court adjourned!" A bang came through the line. I don't know if she just hung up the phone really loudly, or if she was actually sitting there on the phone with a gavel.

Here's the real payoff, though: after my court case, I noticed the wording on the transit website had changed. It now said, "Pass expires on the first of the next month."

Yeah, no duh, thinks pretty much everyone who reads it.

But remember, every time you see a label or warning sign or disclaimer telling you something that seems incredibly obvious, it's there because someone, somewhere, tried to do that thing. The label on the Windex telling you not to drink it? It's there because someone tried to drink Windex.

I can proudly say that I am that person for the Metropass instructions on the TTC website.

What They Said vs. What They Meant

Most of us with ASD learn quickly that neurotypical people don't always say exactly what they mean. This is especially evident over texts. In case you need help decoding everyday exchanges like I do, I've put together a guide.

WHAT THEY SAID	WHAT THEY MEANT
"Don't take offense, but …"	"I've now adequately prepared you for offense. Commencing offense… now!"
"I'm on my way, I'll be there soon."	"Your friend is asleep. This is his mother."
"Sorry, I've got a cold."	"I'm hanging out with someone else."
"Running late. Will get there before the trailers."	"I will arrive one hour into the movie with some guy I just invited."
"This is going to hurt me a lot more than it's going to hurt you."	"This will be agony."

On the day of my nineteenth birthday, I strolled to the bus stop, a little too cocky, Metropass in hand. I was alone, save for three other people. The first two: an elderly couple, unsure as to how the transit system worked. And the third: a man in a vest that said "Info" across the chest, breaking down the many potentially confusing intricacies of the TTC.

We locked eyes and I realized it was one of the transit cops who had busted me in the first place. It didn't feel karmic; instead a little sad. Why should he be the fall guy for a broken system?

In any case, I wouldn't take this for granted. Independence is great, but when you're young, you usually mistake "knowing everything" for being "a know-it-all." It's not bad to ask for help, even if it's after you need help up from slipping on a proverbial banana.

Chapter 13

HERE TODAY, IMPROV TOMORROW

On the night of my very first improv class, many thoughts ran through my head.

"Say something clever. Be funny. Make people like you!" Come to think of it, these thoughts are no different from the thoughts I've had about every social interaction before or since. That night in particular, though, I really should've ignored them.

For those not familiar, improv is basically unscripted theater. Often, the audience gives you a prompt that you then build a scene around. It's crucial in improv to listen to your scene partners, be responsive to them, and go with the flow. When you do that, real magic can happen.

But when I got onstage to do my first scene, I didn't do any of those things. I ignored my scene partner and my brain went on autopilot, and by "autopilot," I mean it defaulted to making "what's the deal with airline food?"–level observational jokes.

I was embarrassed and wanted to go home. The teacher told me I should "act natural," but I was incapable of doing that. Up until then, every conversation I had had been scripted. Penned by Ma and Pa McCreary, and unconvincingly performed by yours truly.

But luckily my fear of failure was dwarfed by my fear of being disliked. I stuck around. In fact, I did three more scenes. Each one less awful than the last. I was learning. More than that, I was catching up on a decade's worth of social misunderstanding. A conversation is like a relationship. It's built on trust, and both parties must be engaged.

Improv taught me more about social skills than any learning strategies class ever could. It got me out of my comfort zone and taught me how to be more flexible. Improv taught me not to fear failure. Which was convenient, because it turned out that after all that, I still wasn't very good at improv.

Still, while I was never a virtuoso of the craft, improv helped define what became my core philosophy: "Life is too short to be a chore, so why not say yes and have fun with it?"

> **A conversation is like a relationship. It's built on trust, and both parties must be engaged.**

I took some of my own advice and finally moved down to Toronto for good. No more taking the Can-Ar bus from home every morning at 6:00 a.m. I boxed up all of my notebooks, napkins, receipts, Pizza Pizza coupons, and anything else I could write a joke on, and moved into Kensington Market.

Kensington Market is like a bohemian fairy-tale land where they sell falafels on every corner and nobody owns a carbon monoxide alarm. I roomed with a delightful, eccentric woman who sold real estate during the day and painted angry anti-iPhone murals at night.

I usually spent my mornings mucking about with her cat, Sadie, who might have actually been a cloud. But in the evenings, I was trying to sharpen my tools down at the Second City Training Centre. By this point, I had graduated from the first two levels in their improv comedy program. I hadn't realized that those were the last of the easy ones and anything beyond that point was for people who lived and breathed improv.

Although I struggled with the form, I couldn't help but fall in love with Toronto's improv community. There was no ego, and people looked out for each other. A typical improv show would end like a *Scooby-Doo* episode, with everyone crying out, "We did it, gang!"

The energy around improv was intoxicating, but after the initial thrill, my interest in it started to wane. I still enjoyed watching the pros do their thing, but I didn't love doing it myself. I hated the uncertainty. All the second-guessing. Once again, that nagging feeling came back to haunt me: "Say yes to life …" But this time, there was a little something extra: "You can't say no."

Partly, it was just a way to do *something*. I wasn't performing stand-up at the time, because I hadn't been able to score any gigs in the city. And to me, if I wasn't performing, it meant I had no value. In my fragile mind, I believed that everyone in society had to contribute something, and if a performer couldn't perform, what were they good for? So I said yes to everything I was offered. I formed a troupe with some of my best friends from Second City and we began producing a twice monthly improv show.

I received some invaluable experience from working on that show. My friends taught me a lot about marketing myself, engaging with a crowd, and collaborating with guests. These lessons helped me a lot at my next gig. Which, as it turned out, had nothing to do with performing and everything to do with improvising.

Summer was coming up, and I was still unable to book any stand-up gigs, so the friends in my troupe suggested it was the perfect time to audition for Second City's highly respected conservatory program. This is where a troupe of ten or so improvisers work over the course of year to put on a show for the main stage. I went to the pre-audition workshop, but then dipped on the audition itself. The half-truth was that I had a summer job that would have made it impossible for me to come in to class. The other half of that truth was that I figured I just wasn't good enough to make it.

My summer job was a bit of a throwback. It was at the film camp I wouldn't shut up about earlier. (I loved that place. Still do.) I applied for the position of counselor and went into the interview reverent, but self-assured. But the interview took a turn when my soon-to-be boss asked, "Would you be open to other positions besides counselor?" And, for the reason explained earlier, I said, "Sure, why not?"

On one hand, this job would have me serving as the camp's videographer, filming all of the summer's major events. On the other hand, it required me to spend my mornings calculating what the campers had spent on candy and counting our inventory of craft supplies and camp merchandise. In other words, they wanted me to do math.

To put it lightly, I suck at math. I am a living debunking of the stereotype that autistic people are mathematical geniuses. How bad am I? I'm so bad at math, my tutor at Kumon told me, "I think we should see other people."

When I aired some of my concerns, my boss tried to assuage them by saying, "We'll be giving you a calculator." A calculator would not save camp from my incompetence. But the boss was so eager to have me aboard that she let me take the night to think it over.

I told my folks about the position. Despite my obvious mathematical concerns, they insisted I go. They even had a compelling argument: "What's fourteen divided by two?"

I said, "Seven?"

"It'll be easier than that," they said. So I took the job.

I arrived at camp with a nostalgia not many people would have for their new workplace. I noted the vast open plains, the tire wall that should have been condemned years ago, and the legion of bucket-hatted counselors, several of them my former counselors, doing cool handshakes and playing guitar in the common area. I breathed in the muggy air: it smelled like home.

We settled in for the night. Even though I wasn't a counselor myself, I still roomed with my peers in the male dorm. The counselors all slept in tiny cubicles in this otherwise big open space, whereas I and Neil, my roommate, slept in a tiny linen closet in the back.

Neil very quickly brushed past the fact that only a summer ago, he was ordering me to go bed by eleven, and embraced me as his friend. Now we stayed up way past eleven together and watched *Battlestar Galactica* on his laptop. Frankly, I needed this kind of friendship because, being on this side of the camp experience for the first time, and not being an actual counselor, I couldn't help but feel like an outsider. Most of the staff knew me as the loud kid who was so neurotic that, true story, in his first of year of camp, he thought he'd accidentally lost his soul in a game of Uno. I knew I had to prove myself and, in the meantime, accept that I would always get a slice of cake last whenever it was someone else's birthday.

We were three days away from the beginning of camp, and I had just been given the rundown of what was required of me every day for the rest of the summer. Clean the craft shop, run the tuck shop, check the merchandise bin to make sure nothing's been lost. It was my first real job as an adult, and I was keen to do it well. Neil Gaiman once said: "You have to be on time, easy to work with, and good at what you do. If you are two out of three of these, you'll be fine." Well, my boss said the craft shop was cleaner than it had ever been and the tuck shop was never on fire, so … I was one and a half?

One night before the campers arrived, I was sweeping up the tuck shop when my bosses gave me my first of many assignments. "Fit all of these cases of pop into the fridge. They have to be nice and cold for when the campers arrive tomorrow," they explained. But here's what my brain picked up from that: "Keep ALL of the pop in a COLD place."

I was able to stuff eight out of ten of the cases into the fridge, and the final two just barely fit into the freezer. What happened next would have been completely avoided had I never opted out of chemistry class for environmental sciences.

Later in the day, to toast the new summer, Neil thought it'd be fair that we grab two root beers from the tuck shop. I insisted he cue up another episode of *Battlestar Galactica* while

I grabbed the drinks. I returned to the tuck shop only to find a sinister dripping coming from the freezer. Before I could even assume the worst, I forced the door open and found the walls of the freezer caked in orange slush and tin shrapnel.

A more rational person might have owned up to the mistake, but in my paranoid little brain, I figured that a goof right out of the gate might lose me my job, as well as the respect of my employers, my peers, and my folks, who must have hoped I'd learned a thing or two after they bailed me out of my last jam with the TTC. My facade of competence would not be cracked by this faux pas. I would not let a sticky freezer be my legacy!

I heard footsteps and shut the freezer without a second thought. My boss poked her head in through the shop's nook, curious as to why I was there at a quarter to eleven. I explained to her that some of the counselors wanted to celebrate, so I was in there grabbing them a drink. She bought it and left. So began the first in a series of Hitchcockian set pieces.

I ran across the camp to the craft shop only to find it locked. Apparently my boss had been working her way across camp, locking each of the shops as she went. I needed paper towels fast. I booked it to the nearest washroom only to find that there was nothing but hand dryers in there. I winced as I spied my boss conversing with one of the groundskeepers not five yards away from the tuck shop.

I darted into the nearest bush and crept back to the male dorm. Doing my best impression of a guy not having a panic attack, I stumbled back into the linen closet I called home and explained to Neil that tuck was closed, and I was going to have a shower instead. He shrugged, a tad disappointed, and tuned into the season one *Battlestar* finale as I grabbed a towel and hurried back to the tuck shop.

My boss was still chatting it up with the groundskeeper. As I walked by, I explained that we were down a few pops and I had to run back to get extras. I slipped in the door behind the two, who were none the wiser that on the other side, I'd whipped my towel out from under my shirt and begun wiping down the freezer. My towel had become an orange-stained mess. My boss knocked on the door and warned me that she'd be locking up in a second. I hid my towel in the nearest trash bin and grabbed two root beers from the fridge.

I opened the door, gestured to the cans, and explained why I took so long. "I forgot what brand they liked." She chuckled and locked the door. I returned to Neil and tossed him the can. He didn't think twice about it, and we toasted to the summer.

That was my first screwup, but by no means my last. And, unfortunately, it was the only one I got away with.

The first of the summer's four sessions of camp was almost over, and it seemed to be going fine. I'd proved myself a valuable asset as a performer for the camp's many spirit suppers and evening programs. And I could be counted on to step in as a counselor when need be. Even the footage I'd shot for the camp was turning out okay. I was feeling so good about things that I had neglected to consider the obvious: my math still sucked. And in my hurried state to get so many things done at once, I didn't bother to double-check it.

The Autistic Brain

The autistic brain is a strange and wondrous place. Some people like to say, "It's just a different operating system." It's better than neurotypical brains at some things and not so good with others. Our brains tend to have a few more glitches due to an error in the hardwiring, so we have to reroute stuff and I don't really know where I'm going with this analogy because I know nothing about computers, which is weird, because I thought we were supposed to be good at this computer stuff and … I think I'll just phone a tech.

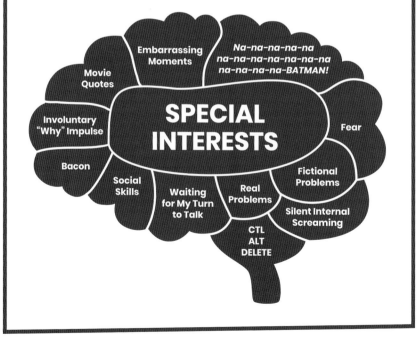

One morning, I came to breakfast and was blindsided with a serious talk from my superiors. It turned out my inventory and spending sheets were a disaster. My numbers were all wrong. They weren't mad, though, or even disappointed. They were just mystified as to how fundamentally wrong my math was.

Given that this was a kind of arts camp, they didn't believe in punishment. Instead, they wanted to work with me on strategies to help me improve. It turned out there were things that could help me do better at math. I told them that the tiny print and the horizontal layout of the numbers was too hard for my brain to register. So they replaced the charts they'd given me with a vertical list that my brain could follow. In a matter of days, my math improved.

I made mistakes again over the next few weeks. But any time a problem came up, my superiors were more than eager to help me through it. Which, in turn, was helping me make more confident decisions. But then it all came to a halt at the end of the second session with what I was convinced was my final screwup.

Prior to every session, incoming campers typically place an order for some kind of camp paraphernalia, like a shirt or hat. Part of my job was to place those items in a bin labelled "Pre-Ordered" so as to not accidentally sell them during the previous session. But on the last day of session two, parents flocked to the tuck shop, cash in hand, demanding camp merchandise.

We blew through everything so quickly that I, in a moment of panic, accidentally sold a few of the articles from the "Pre-Ordered" bin. When I told my boss what had happened, he didn't speak to me for the rest of the day.

This set the tone for session three. I didn't cope well with failure and was beginning to withdraw. One of my colleagues in the office, who had previously been my chief ally, began to find me something of a nuisance. They even came into the tuck shop after hours to rearrange its layout, which, what with me having an autistic mind, made it difficult to find things. Finding things is the only thing I'm worse at than math.

Initially, I felt like I deserved it. It was a kind of cosmic punishment for my many kerfuffles, and my overreliance on authority figures. I could have just sulked my way through the rest of the summer. But then I remembered that creed: "Life's too short to be a chore." *It's never too late to fix things*, I told myself. I confronted my coworker over rearranging the shop, and they were endlessly apologetic. We ended up performing together in the talent show three nights later.

I got back in the saddle and began really cleaning up the craft shop. I collected all of the lost craft supplies left around camp. I coordinated a series of interviews with campers and counselors alike where they stated what made camp so special. I disinfected the entire camp with Lysol while grooving to Fatboy Slim's "Weapon of Choice." And after a long day of work, I said no to the biweekly counselor award ceremonies because it was already 10:00 p.m. and I can only function on at least nine hours of sleep.

Just in time for session four, I had taken back control of my summer, and, better than that, learned a valuable lesson. You should say yes to life when it benefits you and those you care about, but you always have the right to say no when it doesn't.

I worked for two more summers at that camp, each year improving upon the last, becoming more and more competent and confident in myself. At the end of my last summer, I was given a send-off by the entire camp. I can no longer make fun of cheesy endings in movies like *Mr. Holland's Opus*, because that actually happened to me. I said goodbye to all the dorms, and to my roommate, Neil. Most memorably, I bid farewell to my boss, who refused to let me finish my goodbye, because she didn't want to hear me say it. I learned a lot about who I was there, but, sad though it might have been, I had to say goodbye to that part of my life.

I came back to Toronto with a newfound optimism. I hadn't performed improv in quite some time, and frankly, didn't want to. But I approached my old improv buddies with a proposition: "I want to come back to the troupe, but if so, can I host your shows instead?" They let me know that the door was wide open.

Chapter 14

THE TEMPLE GRANDIN SAGA

Coming off my cross-Canada tour, I had felt proud to be an advocate for the ASD community. With a few exceptions, among them the great Adam Schwartz and the Asperger's Are Us troupe, there hasn't been a lot of autistic representation in the comedy world. With that in mind, I was proud to embrace the title of "Aspie Comic."

But I knew that if I were to become a liaison between the autism and comedy communities, I'd have to accept some serious responsibilities. One such responsibility: not looking like a complete doofus in front of the autism scene's most esteemed speaker. I'd now like to tell you about my adventures with the great Dr. Temple Grandin, the Elvis of the autism world.

If you're unfamiliar with Dr. Grandin's work, I'd suggest you do yourself a favor and watch *Temple Grandin*, the HBO movie based on her life. A revolutionary figure in the world of agriculture, and even more influential in the world of autism, Dr. Grandin has been rightfully lauded for her many talks on the state of autistic employment and how we can provide better opportunities for the spectrum's next generation.

But, at seven years old, I didn't know any of that. I was just a snot-nosed kid helping his mom sell Fidget Kits (a pencil case filled with sensory toys; my mom's idea) in the overcrowded basement level of the Metro Toronto Convention Centre. I helped by demonstrating the functionality of the toys, specifically the finger traps, which I had stuck to each of my fingers. We sold hundreds.

Unexpectedly, Dr. Grandin, who'd just finished her talk, came over to our booth looking intrigued. My mom, seizing the day, insisted she take a Fidget Kit on the house. Now, I was a little distracted trying to dislodge my fingers from the finger traps, but apparently, after receiving her sample, Dr. Grandin raised her eyebrows, opened the kit, and took all the toys she liked best.

Flash forward a decade. I'm back in the Metro Toronto Convention Centre. The good people at the Geneva Centre for Autism had asked me to perform a set to close out their conference. Then I hear that I'll actually be opening for Temple

Grandin, and suddenly, I flash back to the first time we met. I'll admit, I was intimidated.

The show, however, goes over quite well. Even Dr. Grandin joins in with the applause. My mom figures that this will be my "in" with her. After Dr. Grandin's closing address, mobs of fans rush the stage. Assuming she's overwhelmed, I go backstage to join my folks. My mom, however, has a digital camera in her hand. "At least get a picture with her," she says.

My mom bellows, "Temple!" The crowd parts, enabling me to walk through, hat in hand, like a bashful newsie. "Temple," I croak, "it was a pleasure getting to work with you. Could I please get a photo?" Here is the resulting photo:

To add insult to injury, as I'm leaving, I hear another fan approach her. They ask, "Do you prefer to be called Temple, or Miss Grandin?"

"Doctor," she replies. And fair enough—Dr. Grandin has worked hard for her title and deserves all the respect that comes with it. But I'd just called her Temple. Twice. To her face.

Although I may have been reading too much into our meeting, at this moment I got the crushing, dejected feeling that one of my heroes thought there was an outside chance I was a moron. I hope she'll forget the whole thing, and, lucky for me, she did.

Three years later, I'm on a plane to the Yukon Territory for another autism conference. The show is in Whitehorse, the capital. Beautiful city, beautiful people, but one catch: there are grizzly bears everywhere. Don't believe me? My interview with the local radio station was interrupted by this announcement: "Sadly, the high school triathlon will be postponed as the race track is now covered in bears."

But let me get to the point. At this gig I'd be opening for, who else, Dr. Temple Grandin. Technically, I'd be opening for her twice. Once in the morning as part of a pre-lunch breakout session, and once at night as part of a show.

A creature of habit, I always forget to pack something. This time it was my show clothes. For the morning, I had to perform in jeans and a ratty brown hoodie. This led to the first words Dr. Grandin and I had exchanged in three years.

"You're eccentric," she says. "That's good. I'm a little eccentric. But this ..." she says, gesturing to my attire, "is unacceptable."

Now, Temple Grandin is famous for her unique fashion style of tailored, bedazzled cowboy shirts. Temple Grandin would never be caught dead in a ratty hoodie. Wanting to save face, I explain, "The airline lost my suit."

She thinks on this. "Oh . . . if you don't want to lose something, don't bring it on a plane." For the time being, my face is safe.

But we still have one more show to do, and luckily, I find a suit for the evening. I come out onstage to a packed room clad in a bright-pink, tasseled, rhinestone shirt. I explain to the crowd, "Temple Grandin gave me some fashion tips." The audience goes nuts, and after the show, Dr. Grandin approaches me.

"Did you buy that because of me?" she asks. "I want it!"

We bond over a plate of nachos back in the green room. It's quite late by that point, but in the Yukon, you'd never know because the sun is always out. She gives me invaluable advice, including tips on how to manage work anxiety and improve my stage presence. But being a pop-culture geek, what will always stick out in my mind is her scathing critique of the Dark Knight film series.

"Batman's gotten real nasty. He's so caught up in punishing criminals that he's forgotten how to save lives. Also, I miss that theme song." Then she sang the theme song from the old Adam West *Batman* show.

> **An advocate can be a carefree prankster, and a comic can be a deep-thinking philosopher. Your job does not define you. A nice lesson, even if it took me three times to learn it.**

This moment stuck with me. Not just because of the cognitive dissonance of watching one of Earth's greatest minds sing the theme to a 1960s kids' show. But because I saw the line between the autism and comedy worlds instantly dissolve. An advocate can be a carefree prankster, and a comic can be a deep-thinking philosopher. Your job does not define you. A nice lesson, even if it took me three times to learn it.

Chapter 15

THE BROTHERS STIM

You might see an autistic person flapping their hands or repeating words or sounds and be curious about that. This is called self-stimulatory behavior, and in the autism community we call it "stimming."

Stimming is an adaptive behavior that helps people cope with both positive and negative emotions. My brother Matty likes to flap his hands around when he's excited. I crack my knuckles next to my ear when I'm nervous. If you're getting too much sensory input, stimming can help block it out. Or it can provide extra sensory input when it's needed.

Some types of stimming can be a bit off-putting to neurotypicals, but believe me, we're more afraid of you than you are of us. Nothing scares autistic people quite like this kind of announcement on the subway: "If you notice any strange or suspicious behavior, please report it to security …"

Don't Stop the Stim!

"Stims" come in many shapes and sizes: staring at lights, repetitive blinking, moving your fingers in front of your eyes, tapping your ears, snapping your fingers, making sounds, spinning objects, rubbing your skin, scratching, smelling objects, rocking, jumping, clapping, or leg-shaking.

A stim might indicate that someone has a problem, but the stim itself is not the problem. In fact, asking an autistic person not to stim can end up causing more problems than the stim itself.

When we were kids, one of my brother's greatest struggles was going out in public because the only way he could communicate was through a sort of falsetto wailing. Speaking of things that draw attention on the subway—there's nothing worse for an autistic child or their parent than to have all eyes whip toward you and strangers approach you with unsolicited advice. As he grew up, Matthew did learn how to use sign language, but by the time he turned eighteen, he had retained only two signs: the one for "toilet" and the one for "cookie." But he did have more than one stim that changed the way I related to him.

After I'd moved out, I didn't stop visiting home entirely. Every other week, I'd hitch a bus ride back to Orangeville to meet up with my folks and jam with the local jazz band. Of course, I'd be staying at my folks' place. Which I dreaded, in that I might not get any sleep. My little brother's sleep schedule

had only worsened since he'd gotten out of high school, and in that time, he'd become more manic in his nightly escapades.

In half-hour intervals, he'd kick me out of my bed so he could sleep in it, then once I was comfy on the couch, he'd boot me off that. But usually, if he got you up, it was a ruse to get you to switch the VHS tapes in his VCR. He couldn't seem to stand watching a movie (usually a Disney Sing Along Songs tape) for more than five minutes at a time.

I began refusing to perform these tasks for him, feeling like if I put my foot down and stood up to him, he'd stop. He didn't. This behavior was getting worse and I began finding more and more reasons to distance myself from my old home. For a time, I turned my back on what was, for most of my life, my idea of normal.

Meanwhile, my older brother, Andrew, was working toward becoming a social worker. He was doing excellent work with Matthew, taking him on trips and such. I envied their connection, because the only one I seemed to have with my little bro was one where I'd fold my arms in defiance and he'd yell and stamp his feet at me. Space seemed to be best for both of us.

My dad and I flew down to Boston in the spring of 2016. We were brought out there so I could perform at a unique function: a weekend-long group therapy session for autism families. I was intrigued. I opened the conference on the Saturday morning. There was a lot to do and see in Boston, and yet, I wanted to stick around to see what this show was all about. Frankly, after about half an hour, I had to jump ship.

It was just a little too … introspective for me. I'm a comic. I'm supposed to make the internal external. This was a little more in the vein of guided meditation.

But I did come back on the Sunday, which was structured far more like a town hall meeting. A Q&A where families (typically, neurotypical parents and autistic children) could vent their concerns. Before I could even raise my hand, one family had already asked my question: "My kids can only connect with me through me performing a task for them. What do I do?"

The moderator responded: "People want a connection on their own terms. If you can replace that task with something you both enjoy, maybe you could find a better connection."

My brain imploded. *All of those times my brother wanted me to swap out a tape was just him trying to be a part of my life? I'm such an idiot!* Which is something I only wish I had thought to myself, but actually I blurted it out in a moment of clarity. Like I said, I'm not so good with internal—only external. Luckily, I was in the least judgmental room on the planet, but I had accidentally kicked off an "I am Spartacus"–like wave of parents standing up and screaming out their own epiphanies. (They liked me there. I would go on to do eight more of these conferences.)

On the plane back home, I made a mental list of things Matthew likes, to try to find activities I could share with him. *Cannonballing into the pool? It's March, that's too cold. Driving in the car? Nope! I don't and should never have a license … Jumping on the trampoline? That's worth a shot.*

When we got home, I went to give Matthew my customary greeting, in response to which he customarily brushed past me and dragged my Dad into the living room, wanting him to swap out the *101 Dalmatians* sing-along VHS for *The Aristocats* sing-along. I tried to get my brother's attention by calling his name and gesturing to the trampoline, but he wouldn't budge. At that point, I knew I just had to go out and do it. It didn't take long for him to follow me outside.

All of those times my brother wanted me to swap out a tape was just him trying to be a part of my life? I'm such an idiot!

Matthew wandered out into the backyard just in time to find me severing a few vertebrae screwing up a backflip. He hopped on, and we bounced for an hour straight, which, in hindsight, wasn't good for the crick in my neck, but it didn't matter. Even if it hurt to go to sleep that night, at least I wasn't up because my brother kicked me out of bed.

I began coming back to my folks' place more and more regularly. I used any chance I could to hang out with my little bro. I'd ride in the car with him and my dad. My dad liked to drive with the radio on, but my brother had full control of what we listened to. Any time my dad and I got to talking too much and he felt left out, he'd tap on my shoulder to get me to change the channel. It felt far more endearing now.

Chapter 16

GENERATOR 2: JUDGMENT DAY

When I was much younger, before I'd even begun doing stand-up, my dad took my older brother and me to see Billy Connolly, one of the greatest comedians of all time, at Massey Hall.

The show was phenomenal, but there were long stretches where I couldn't help but fantasize about being on that stage myself. Honestly, I never anticipated it coming sooner rather than later.

It was the fall of 2016 and I had started to gain some traction in the autism scene. I made fast friends with a former producer at the CBC, Canada's national broadcaster, who ultimately scored me a gig at the annual Geneva Symposium, a conference for autism in Toronto.

I discovered an unexpected bit of karma when I looked at the program. I was going to be performing at the same time as, and right next door to, Dr. S., the man who had diagnosed me with autism all those years ago.

When I got up onstage, I pointed this out to the audience, feeling like I needed to acknowledge the coincidence somehow. I wanted to tell them how much his diagnosis had meant to me, how important his compassion and wisdom had been in helping me develop into the person I had become.

There were many things I could have said, but the words I chose to bellow at the wall where Dr. S. was speaking in the next room were: "Look at your creation!"

It was one of the most cathartic moments of my young life.

The Geneva show was a hit, and the producer continued helping me along. My next gig was at an autism gala event, where a crew of reporters were going to be following me around the day before the show, filming my creative process and my daily routine, which is:

I wake up at 8:00 a.m. At 8:10: I shower. 8:15: I have breakfast. 8:22: I brush my teeth. 8:24: If there are no classes or work obligations, I go for a run. I've started my days this way since I was in grade five. No day is ever quite the same, but I feel safer knowing there is a routine for me to fall back on. If class is cancelled, there is a theater a block away from my school where I can catch a flick. If I get bumped from my gig at the local comedy club, there is a theater a block away from the bar where I can catch a flick. If my friend leaves me hanging at the theater, there is a theater a block away from the theater where I can catch a flick.

Routines exist everywhere. I have a routine for my meals (two eggs over easy and a bagel), my pastimes (any movie under two hours at any theater that's not a Cineplex), and my job (pace and recite the first three jokes of my set). Routine means everything for us autistic folk, and breaking from it can be quite stressful.

Even though it was anything but routine to have a film crew follow me around, the show itself went great, as did the interviews. Or so I thought.

When I finally saw my interview, I couldn't help but feel misrepresented. The interview was cobbled together with several inserts of my shaking hands and feet, and a sorrowful narration that implies I am barely able to function and comedy is the only thing that motivates me to live. And while all those things might be true, I knew for a fact that I could hold my own in an interview.

I went to air my frustrations to the producer, but before I could, she told me that she'd just scored me a spot on CBC's *Accent on Toronto*, a showcase for the city's best newcomer and veteran comics. I kept my mouth shut, and figured this would be a better way to salvage my reputation. I could prove that I wasn't just an "autistic comic," but could make a real impression in the mainstream comedy scene.

It's mid-October, the night of the show. I just finished having dinner with my folks, which I didn't eat because, for the first time since I was fourteen, I feel real fear about performing. I know the material I've been using works with an autism crowd, but I don't know how a predominantly neurotypical crowd will respond. To make matters worse, the whole thing is being recorded live, so if I mess up, it will be out there for eternity. And to top it off, I'm following Arthur Simeon and Eman El-Husseini, two of the funniest comics working today. Honestly, I'm terrified.

I get to the venue early. The mic check goes smoothly. The tech guys warn me that the spotlight will not move with me and I have to stay directly under it if I want to be seen at all, which makes me feel relieved that, if I bomb, I'll only need to sidestep in any direction to completely disappear.

I spend the next ninety minutes staring at a wall backstage. The show begins. Once I hear people laughing, I feel a bit relieved. They're a nice crowd. But then again, the people making them laugh are world-class comedians. More doubt settles in. Halfway through Eman's set, I'm given the pep talk of a lifetime from an unexpected source.

The comedian Dave Hemstad has come to hang with some of the comics backstage during the show. He shoots a quick glance at me. Probably thinks, *Why is there a twelve-year-old back here?* and wants to clear things up. He sees me shaking and asks, "You up next?"

I say, "Yeah."

He asks, "First time here?"

I say, "Yeah."

"What's the worst gig you've ever done?" I tell him about that one stop on the tour where no one had laughed. He smiles.

"Want to prove them all wrong?"

I nod earnestly. He grabs me by the hand and flings me off my stoop. "Then go out there and kill it!"

Not a second later, my name is called to the stage and I run out there to grab the mic. The show goes off without a hitch, and before I know it, twelve minutes have passed by like nothing. I leave the stage a little light-headed. The other comics mosey over to say congrats. For the rest of the night, I feel if not like a king, then a court jester who was spared decapitation.

The next morning, the fear returned. My dad called. Evan Hadfield, the son of astronaut Colonel Chris Hadfield, had seen the show and wanted me to perform that same set on his show Generator at Massey Hall—a showcase for music, comedy, and ideas that features some famous and incredibly brilliant people. But before that, he wanted to me to meet with him. At his dad's place. With his dad there. Along with a handful of the other performers (among the ones not present, *Mythbusters'* Adam Savage and author Neil Gaiman).

The Hadfields are a lovely family who live in a home a

little less Jetsons-y than I would've hoped. Chris Hadfield was there talking about the music set list with the band, Tupper Ware Remix Party, and also discussing the next stage of human evolution with two literal cyborgs. It was in that moment that I came down with what is commonly referred to as imposter syndrome—an inability to recognize your own accomplishments and a persistent fear of being exposed as a fraud. Thankfully, I was able to vent this feeling to a few of the band members, who were incredibly sympathetic. It turns out many, if not most creative people experience this feeling.

> **For the rest of the night, I feel if not like a king, then like a court jester who was spared decapitation.**

Once again, on the night of the performance, I had dinner with my folks, but I didn't really have dinner. I was a little less nauseous now that I knew my material would fly with a neurotypical audience, but given the more cerebral crowd Chris Hadfield tended to attract, I was worried the response to my set wouldn't be met with laughter, but with icy analysis, like students watching surgery in a nineteenth-century hospital.

I was stupid to even think this, given that it was a variety show, but it was hard to not feel out of place when I was on the docket with a guy two years younger than me who has a plan to get rid of the trash pile in the Pacific Ocean. But I figured the MC, Adam Savage, had my back, being no stranger to lighthearted fun.

Chris Hadfield introduced me to Adam Savage before the show, and I'll never forget this moment. He shook my hand and proclaimed: "You! After the show, I want to work with you!"

I was caught off guard. "Really?"

"Yep! I think you and I can change the world."

Beyond flattered, I quipped, "Give me a date and time and we'll make it happen."

"I mean it, man. Between you and me, we can finally get rid of that garbage pile in the Pacific."

A beat. Chris explains, "This is Michael ... the comedian."

"Oh ... well, they're gonna love you ...," Adam replies ... and leaves.

I cherish this memory fondly.

It's finally my time to get onstage. The audience is howling from Savage's opening monologue. I come out to center stage and for a moment get lost in the weirdness of the whole situation. To the right of me, Tupper Ware Remix Party, clad in neon spandex, is laying down a funky bass line. About a meter to the left of me, all the performers and speakers are chilling on a couch, bobbing their heads to the music. And somewhere up in the rafters, I spied the very seat I sat in seven years ago when I saw Billy Connolly. It was now occupied by some kid who could very well have been daydreaming about getting on this stage someday.

For a moment, time slowed to a crawl, and then I told my first joke, and it's like the next twelve minutes didn't happen. It's a surreal feeling, finally getting the very thing that you want, and losing it almost instantaneously. I sat on the couch next to Chris Hadfield and watched the cyborgs dance to vibrations in the earth that only they could feel. I started to think about my next goal: getting back on the Massey Hall stage.

After the show I bumped into Neil Gaiman, who was kind enough to let me ask him some questions about the Sandman series. He gave me some life advice, too. Now, I'm paraphrasing, but the gist of it was: "Make every show a Massey Hall show. The venue's history doesn't matter. The size of the crowd or the stage doesn't matter. Just make it an event you can be proud of."

After that night, I performed for about fifty people in a basement in Woodstock. It was the best show of my life. At least, until the next one came along.

Epilogue

It's 2019 and I'm rooming with my best friend from high school. When he isn't cleaning horse stables, we're hitting up open mics together.

The documentary I shot for the tour is still in the works. It's shaping up to be a decades-long epic. A friend of mine from camp has bravely taken over directorial duties. A release date, a running time, and a plot have yet to be determined.

I'm dating someone who's also on the spectrum. We're looking to buy a pet. We're thinking of getting a cockatoo because it reminds me of myself. It's very loud.

Writing an epilogue is hard, especially when your story is not even close to finished. When I wrote the first draft of this, I said, "I don't go back to Orangeville much, but when I do, my little brother and I have a blast bouncing on the trampoline. We've gone through about four now."

And then something terrible happened.

In the spring of 2018, Matty suffered a grand mal seizure while swimming and drowned. Three months later, my family held a celebration of life in his honor. The event was at my parents' house, and Matty's ashes were buried under a tree in his favorite spot, where his pool used to be. My family's future is still unsettled. His passing has left a huge hole in our world. For now, we just try to live the clichés and take it one day at a time.

I hope this book has been a help to anyone who needs it. In a world like this, all we have left is our ability to empathize. My awkward experiences might not be universal, but I know that the feelings are.

To my neurotypical readers, I appreciate your understanding and your drive to learn.

To my autistic readers, I want to remind you once more, you're not alone.

Acknowledgments

I'd like to thank my family and friends for putting up with me. Thank you to the good people at Annick Press, especially Paula Ayer and Kaela Cadieux, for all of their wisdom and guidance. I would like to give a huge shout out to all the people who have supported me on my Facebook page and everyone who has ever come to one of my shows. Finally, thanks to anyone I've ever had an awkward exchange with. Without you, I would not have had enough material to meet the quota.

Austism Resources

If you're searching for more info on autism, I suggest that you look into any or all of the following organizations. I am not suggesting that any of them will have all the answers you are looking for. You may find that some of them even take some controversial positions. Do what I did: I had a look, applied some critical thinking to what I found, and decided to use what worked for me. Some of these resources will be best suited to those of us who are on the spectrum; some will be better sources of information for parents of the profoundly challenged, like my younger brother; some will help employers understand the capabilities and perspectives of those with autism; and most will provide an overview for those looking to find out more about autism spectrum disorder.

Autism Canada – https://autismcanada.org/

Autism Ontario – http://www.autismontario.com/

Autism Society of America – http://www.autism-society.org/

Autistic Self Advocacy Network – http://autisticadvocacy.org/

Geneva Centre for Autism – https://www.autism.net/

National Autistic Society – https://www.autism.org.uk/

Specialisterne Canada – http://ca.specialisterne.com/